AN ADAPTED CL

Frankenstein

Mary Shelley

GLOBE FEARON
EDUCATIONAL PUBLISHER

PARAMUS, NEW JERSEY

Paramount Publishing

Executive Editor: Barbara Levadi
Adapter: Emily Hutchinson
Senior Editor: Bernice Golden
Editorial Assistant: Roger Weisman
Art Director: Nancy Sharkey
Cover and Interior Illustrations: Carlotta A. Tormey
Production Editor: Linda Greenberg
Electronic Systems Specialist: José López
Marketing Manager: Sandra Hutchison

ISBN: 0-835-91116-0

Printed in the United States of America.
3 4 5 6 7 8 9 10 99 98

GLOBE FEARON
EDUCATIONAL PUBLISHER
PARAMUS, NEW JERSEY

Paramount Publishing

CONTENTS

ABOUT THE AUTHOR

Mary Shelley was born Mary Wollstonecraft Godwin in London in 1797. She was the daughter of two well-known English writers, William Godwin and Mary Wollstonecraft. Two months before Mary's seventeenth birthday, she ran away with Percy Bysshe Shelley, the famous English poet.

She spent the summer of 1816 in Switzerland with Shelley and some of their friends. It was there that the idea for a ghost story was first suggested to her. The frightening images that formed the basis for her famous novel, *Frankenstein,* came to her one evening. She tells about this experience in her introduction to the novel on page *vii.*

After she and Shelley returned to London in September 1816, they faced a series of disasters. One of Mary's half-sisters committed suicide. This was soon followed by the suicide of Shelley's wife, Harriet. Harriet's death allowed Mary and Shelley to legally marry.

Mary Shelley became a widow in 1822 when her husband drowned, at the age of 29, in a boating accident. She continued to write until her death in 1851. Her other novels include *Valperga* (1823), *The Last Man* (1826), and *Lodore* (1835).

ADAPTER'S NOTE

In preparing this edition of *Frankenstein,* we have kept closely to what Mary Shelley wrote. We have modified some vocabulary and shortened and simplified many sentences and paragraphs. None of the story, however, has been omitted.

PREFACE

Mary Shelly's novel *Frankenstein* introduced one of the most haunting characters in Western literature. The unnamed creature is brought to life by the young Victor Frankenstein, a student working in an isolated laboratory. This story has been the subject of numerous movies, most of which have considerably changed the original plot.

Many people who are familiar with the movie versions are surprised to find that the creature is a sympathetic character in the novel. He is naturally gentle, curious, intelligent, and kind. He wants nothing more than to communicate with the people who reject him. Shunned because of his horrible appearance, he is cut off from all humanity and forced to turn to his creator to solve his problems.

Mary Shelley gave her book a subtitle, *The Modern Prometheus*. This is a reference to the Greek myth of the Titan who stole fire from the gods and gave it to humans. Prometheus, like Frankenstein, was severely punished for his act. Did Shelley mean that the spark of life Victor Frankenstein gave to the creature was something no human should have stolen?

CHARACTERS

Robert Walton . . . . *an explorer*

Margaret Saville . . . . *Robert Walton's sister*

Victor Frankenstein . . . . *a young science student*

Caroline Frankenstein . . . . *Victor's mother*

Alphonse Frankenstein . . . . . *Victor's father, a noble humanitarian*

Elizabeth Lavenza . . . *a girl raised as Victor's sister*

Henry Clerval . . . . *Victor's closest friend*

The Creature . . . . *the unnamed "monster"*

M. De Lacey . . . . *a blind man exiled from Paris*

Felix De Lacey . . . . *the son of M. De Lacey*

Agatha De Lacey . . . . . . *the daughter of M. De Lacey*

Safie . . . . *Felix's fiancée*

Ernest and William . . . . *Victor's brothers*

M. Krempe and M. Waldman . . . . . *science professors*

Mr. Kirwin . . . . *a judge in a coastal town in Ireland*

AUTHOR'S INTRODUCTION

I would like to answer a question often asked of me—"How did you, then a young girl, come to think of so very hideous an idea?"

It is not unusual that, as the daughter of two famous writers, I should very early in life have thought of writing. As a child I scribbled. One of my favorite pastimes was to "write stories." Still I had a dearer pleasure than this. I liked to follow up trains of thought that were based on imaginary incidents.

My dreams were much more fantastic than my writings. When I wrote, I imitated closely what others had done, rather than putting down the suggestions of my own mind. What I wrote was something that others would read. My dreams, however, were all my own. I escaped in them when I was annoyed. They were my dearest pleasure when free.

As a girl I lived mainly in the country and passed a great deal of time in Scotland. I usually stayed on the blank and dreary northern shores near the city of Dundee. Blank and dreary I call them now, but they did not seem so then. They were the only place where I was free to live in my imagination. I wrote then, but in a very ordinary style.

I did not make myself the heroine of my tales. My own life seemed too dull. I didn't believe that romantic woes or wonderful events would ever be my lot.

After this my life became busier, and reality stood in place of fiction. My husband, however, thought that I should write. It wasn't that he thought I could produce anything worth reading. He just wanted to see if I showed any talent worth developing. Still I did nothing. Traveling and my family took up my time.

In the summer of 1816, we visited Switzerland and became the neighbors of Lord Byron. At first we spent pleasant hours on the lake or walking on the shore. Lord Byron was the only one of us who put his thoughts on paper.

But it proved a wet, dreary summer, and constant rain often kept us in the house for days. Some books of ghost stories fell into our hands. I have not seen these stories since then, but I remember them as clearly as if I had read them yesterday.

"We will each write a ghost story," said Lord Byron, and we agreed. There were four of us. Byron began a tale, part of which he printed at the end of one of his poems. Shelley began a poem based on the experiences of his early life. Byron's other friend had some terrible idea about a skull-headed lady, but he never finished his story.

I busied myself *to think of a story*. I wanted one that was at least as good as the ones we had been reading. I wanted one that would speak to our mysterious fears and awaken thrilling horror. I wanted a story that would make the reader afraid to look around. I wanted one that would curdle the blood and quicken the beatings of the heart. If I did not accomplish these things, my ghost story would be unworthy of its name. I thought and thought, but I came up with nothing. *Have you thought of a story?* I was asked each morning. Each morning I was forced to say no.

Everything must have a beginning, and that beginning must be linked to something that went before. Invention does not come out of nothing. The materials must, in the first place, be there. Invention can give form to dark, shapeless substances, but it cannot bring into being the substance itself.

Many and long were the conversations between Lord Byron and Shelley. I was a nearly silent listener.

During one of these conversations, the nature of the principle of life was discussed. They wondered whether it would ever be discovered. They wondered if a corpse would ever be brought back to life. Perhaps the various parts of a creature might be made, brought together, and given the spark of life.

Night fell on this talk, and we all retired to rest. When I placed my head on my pillow, I did not sleep, nor could I be said to think. My imagination took over. It brought a vividness to the images that arose in my mind. I imagined the pale student kneeling beside the thing he had put together. I saw the hideous shape of a man stretched out. Then, on the working of some powerful engine, I saw it show signs of life, stirring with an uneasy motion. It was a frightful sight, as would be any human attempt to mock the work of the Creator of the world.

His success would terrify the artist. He would rush away from his terrible work, horror-stricken. He would hope that, left to itself, the slight spark of life he had given would fade. He would hope that the creature would just die. He sleeps, but he is awakened. He opens his eyes and sees the horrid thing standing at his bedside, opening his curtains. It would be looking at him with yellow, watery, but thoughtful eyes.

I opened mine in terror. The idea so took over my mind that a thrill of fear ran through me. O! If only I could write a story that would frighten my reader as I myself had been frightened that night!

Swift as light was the idea that broke in on me. "I have found it! What terrified me will terrify others. I need only describe the ghost that had haunted my midnight pillow." In the morning I announced that I had *thought of a story*. I began that day with the words *It was on a dreary night of November.* Then I just wrote down the grim terrors of my waking dream.

At first I thought of just a few pages, of a short tale. But Shelley urged me to develop the idea into a longer story. I certainly did not owe any part of the story to my husband. But if not for him, it would never have taken its present form.

Now, once again, I bid my hideous creation to go forth and prosper. I like this story, for it was written in happy days when death and grief were but words to me. Its pages remind me of many a walk and many a conversation with one who, in this world, I shall never see again. But this is for myself. My readers have nothing to do with these memories.

M. W. S.
London, October 15, 1831

Opening Letters

Letter 1: To Mrs. Saville, England
St. Petersburg, December 11, 17—

You will be happy to hear that I arrived in St. Petersburg[1] safely. My first task is to assure my dear sister that I am doing well and that I am looking forward to success in my undertaking.

As I walk through the streets, I can feel a cold northern breeze on my face. This breeze, which comes from the North Pole, gives me a delightful taste of what it will be like there. Most people think that the North Pole is a lifeless place of snow and ice. I believe that it is a place of beauty and delight. I am sure that I will find a land more beautiful and wondrous than any other region on earth.

In that country of eternal light, I might discover the power that attracts the compass needle. The idea of being the first person to reach the Pole is enough to help me conquer my fear of danger or death.

I have been dreaming of this adventure since I was a child. Do you remember Uncle Thomas's library? Every book in it was about a voyage of discovery. I did not have an education, and yet I read those books day and night.

I have been preparing myself for this voyage for the past six years. I went on whaling ships to the North Sea several times. I voluntarily experienced cold, famine, thirst, and lack of sleep. I am well prepared for

---

1. **St. Petersburg** a city in Russia at the eastern end of the Gulf of Finland

1

what lies ahead. My courage is firm, but my hopes and spirits are often depressed. I am about to begin a long and difficult voyage, and I will be responsible for the safety of my crew. I know that I am as well prepared as anyone can be. I also know that anything might go wrong.

In two or three weeks, I shall depart for the city of Archangel. There I will hire a ship and find a crew. We will sail in June, but who knows when we shall return? May heaven bless you and help me.

Your loving brother,
Robert Walton

Letter 2: To Mrs. Saville, England
Archangel, March 28, 17—

How slowly the time passes here! We are closed in by frost and snow, and I am in the process of finding a crew. I am greatly looking forward to this adventure, but one thing saddens me. I have no friend to share in my joy. Also if anything goes wrong, I have no one to talk to about it.

I have good sailors, so far, and a good man for a captain. Perhaps he will be the friend I am looking for. He is of a very sensitive nature. I heard this story about him: Some years ago, he was in love with a young woman. Her father had already agreed to their marriage, but the woman told him she loved another man. He was a poor man, and her father would not agree to the marriage. So the captain gave her his entire fortune and the farm where he had hoped to live with her. Then he left so that she could marry the man she loved.

But enough about that. I can hardly wait to get started. We are just waiting for the weather to clear up. Then we will be on our way to unexplored regions. We shall soon see what a poet once called "the land of mist and snow." Please write whenever you can. Perhaps your letters will get to me when I most need to hear from you.

Letter 3: To Mrs. Saville, England
July 7, 17—

I write a few lines in haste to say that I am safe and on my way. This letter will reach England on a ship headed home from Archangel. As we travel north, we see big sheets of floating ice, but this doesn't seem to scare the men. We are now far north, but it is not as cold as you might think. The southern breezes bring us the warmth of England.

Not much has happened so far—nothing worth writing about, anyway. I will be happy indeed if everything continues to go so well. I am not looking for any danger, just for success. I must close this letter now. Heaven bless my dear sister!

Letter 4: To Mrs. Saville, England
August 5, 17—

Something so strange has happened! Six days ago, we were nearly surrounded by ice. It closed in the ship on all sides, leaving hardly enough room for us to float. Our situation was dangerous, for we were also surrounded by a very thick fog. We cast anchor, hoping that a change would soon take place.

About two o'clock, the fog cleared away, and we saw vast plains of ice stretched out in every direction. A strange sight suddenly attracted our attention and made us forget the danger in which we found ourselves. We saw a dogsled about half a mile away. A creature shaped like a man, but of gigantic size, guided the dogs. We watched the rapid progress of the traveler through our telescopes until he was lost in the distance, heading north.

We were hundreds of miles from land. Where could he have come from? About two hours after this, the ice began to break up. We decided to wait until morning before getting started again. We didn't want to hit any large pieces of ice in the dark.

In the morning as soon as it was light, I went on deck. I found all the sailors busy on one side of the ship. They were leaning over, talking to someone in the sea. A dogsled, like the one we had seen before, had drifted toward us on a large piece of ice. Only one dog remained alive, but there was a man in the sled. The sailors were trying to get him to come on board the ship. He was not, as the other traveler seemed to be, a giant from some undiscovered island. He was a European.

He spoke in English, with a foreign accent. "Before I board your ship, will you tell me which way you are going?" he asked.

You can well imagine how surprised I was to hear such a question. After all, this man was in obvious need of help. I would have expected him to be begging us to take him aboard. When I told him we were heading north on a voyage of discovery, he agreed to come on board. His arms and legs were nearly frozen, and his body was terribly thin. He was tired and in pain. We tried to carry him into the cabin, but as soon as he was out of the fresh air, he fainted. So we brought him back on deck, wrapped him in blankets, and fed him some soup. This made him feel better.

After two days, he was able to speak. I moved him into my own cabin. I never saw a more pained man. His eyes looked wild to the point of madness. He was generally melancholy and despairing, as if he carried the woes of the world on his back. But if anyone was kind to him, his whole face lit up.

One of the men finally asked him why he had come so far on the ice in a dogsled. He immediately looked serious and said, "To seek one who fled from me."

"Did the man you were following travel in a dogsled?"

"Yes."

"Then I think we saw him. The day before we picked you up, we saw a dogsled, with a man in it, across the ice."

This got the stranger's attention, and he asked many questions. He wondered if we thought that the other dogsled had been destroyed when the ice broke. I told him that it was impossible to know. Since the ice had broken several hours after we saw him, the other traveler might have had enough time to get to a place of safety.

From then on, the stranger wanted to be on deck so that he could watch for the other dogsled. I told him that he was too weak, but that I would have someone watch for him.

Such is my knowledge about this stranger up to the present day. He has improved in health, but he is very quiet. I am the only one he seems comfortable with. I told you before, dear Margaret, that I wished I had a friend. Perhaps I have found one. I will continue this letter about the stranger whenever I have new things to report.

August 13, 17—

My affection for this stranger increases every day. He is gentle, intelligent, and refined. He is feeling much better now, and he is always on deck, looking out on the ice. We have spoken about my expedition to the Pole. I told him how important it is to me. "One man's life or death is but a small price to pay for the knowledge I am seeking," I told him.

When I said this, a dark gloom spread over his face. He placed his hands over his eyes, and I saw tears trickle fast from between his fingers. Then he groaned, and finally he spoke. "Unhappy man! Do you share my madness? If you knew what I know, you would change your mind."

R. W.

August 19, 17—

Yesterday the stranger said, "I have decided to share with you what I have learned. You seek knowledge and wisdom, as I once did. I hope that it doesn't cost you as much as it has cost me. I have only one more thing to do during my life, and after that my life will be over. I see that you think you can help me. Once you have heard my story, however, you will understand that I am beyond any help."

He will begin his story tomorrow. Each evening, I will write down what he says, using his own words as much as possible. Even now, as I begin my task, his full-toned voice swells in my ears.

1 Victor Frankenstein's Youth

I am by birth a Genevese.[1] My family is one of the most distinguished of that republic. My father was well known for his public service. He was respected by all who knew him. It was not until later in life that he became a husband and the father of a family.

Because the circumstances of his marriage tell something about his character, I will describe them. One of his best friends was a man named Beaufort. He had been a wealthy merchant, but he had fallen into poverty. Too proud to continue living in the same city where he had once been rich and respected, Beaufort moved to a small town. He and his daughter lived there unknown and in wretchedness.

My father loved Beaufort with the truest friendship, and he wanted to help him get back into business. After a search that took ten months, my father found out where he and his daughter were living. He hurried to Beaufort's house, but when he arrived there, misery and despair alone welcomed him.

Beaufort had been unable to find work, and his grief had made him ill. Three months after moving, he lay sick in bed. His daughter, Caroline, had done what she could to take care of him. The small amount of money they had was almost gone. She had found work braiding straw.

Several months passed in this manner. Beaufort

---

1. **Genevese** a resident of Geneva, a city in southwest Switzerland on Lake Geneva

grew worse. In the tenth month he died in Caroline's arms, leaving her an orphan and a beggar. This blow overcame her, and she knelt by Beaufort's coffin, weeping bitterly. Just then, my father entered the room. He came like a protecting spirit to the poor girl, who put herself in his care. He took her to Geneva, where she lived with a relative. Two years after this event, Caroline became his wife.

My parents were very happy together. They spent several years traveling through Italy, Germany, and France. I, their eldest child, was born in Naples and as an infant went with them on their trips. For several years, I was their only child.

When I was about five years old, we spent a week on the shores of Lake Como in Italy. One day, while we were out walking, we passed by the cottage of a poor peasant family. There were five children, but one of them attracted my mother far above all the rest. This child, who appeared to be about my age, was thin and very fair. Her hair was the brightest living gold. It seemed like a crown on her head. Her brow was clear, her blue eyes cloudless. Her lips and face were so sweet that she looked like an angel.

The peasant woman told my mother about the girl. She was not her child, but the daughter of a nobleman. Her mother was a German and had died while giving her birth. The infant had been placed in the care of these good people. No one knew if the child's father was dead or alive.

With my father's permission, my mother persuaded the peasant family to let her take the child. They were fond of the sweet orphan, and they thought it unfair to keep her in such poverty. They talked to their village priest, and the result was that Elizabeth Lavenza moved in with us. She became the beautiful and adored companion of my childhood—more than just a sister.

We were brought up together. There was not quite a year's difference in our ages. We lived in perfect harmony, never fighting or even disagreeing about anything. Elizabeth loved poetry and the beauty of nature. She admired the shapes of the mountains. She delighted in the changes of the seasons and the silence of winter. She found excitement in our Alpine summers. While she was interested in the magnificent appearances of things, I delighted in investigating their causes. The world was to me a secret that I desired to understand.

After the birth of a second son, my junior by seven years, my parents gave up their wandering life. We owned a house in Geneva, and we also had a country home. It was about four miles away, on the eastern shore of the lake. We spent time mainly in the country home. We lived a rather secluded and quiet life.

It was my temper to avoid a crowd and to attach myself to only a few people. My closest friend was Henry Clerval, the son of a merchant in Geneva. He was talented and imaginative. He was deeply read in books of chivalry and romance. He composed songs and wrote many tales of enchantment and knightly adventure. He tried to make us act in plays about knights and heroes.

I had an eager desire to learn. I confess that neither language, government, nor politics held any interest for me. It was the secrets of heaven and earth that I desired to learn.

Clerval, on the other hand, was interested in heroes and adventurers. His dream was to become one of those whose names are recorded in history as being brave and gallant. The saintly soul of Elizabeth was ever there to bless and inspire us. She was the living spirit of love to soften and soothe us.

No human being could have had a happier childhood than I. When I visited other families, I became even more aware of how lucky I was to have such kind and indulgent parents.

I felt great pleasure in these memories of childhood, before misfortune tainted my mind. In speaking of my early days, I remember the birth of the passion that later swept away all my hopes and joys.

When I was 13, I started to read the works of Cornelius Agrippa, Paracelsus, and Albertus Magnus.[2] My father said, "My dear Victor, do not waste your time on these books. They are sad trash." He should have told me that modern science had completely disproved their ideas. If he had, I would have thrown them aside. It is even possible that my thoughts would never have led to my ruin.

As it was, I continued to read these authors. They seemed to me treasures known to few besides myself. I took their words as truth, and I became their disciple. I began to dream of the glory that would be mine if I could banish disease from the human frame.

Nor was this my only vision. The raising of ghosts was a promise freely made by my favorite authors. The fact that I could never do this only made me doubt myself. I thought it was because I lacked experience or had made some mistake. I never once doubted my teachers, until an accident again changed my ideas.

When I was about 15, I saw a violent and terrible

---

2. Cornelius Agrippa, Paracelsus, and Albertus Magnus early scientists, known as alchemists, who tried to create life in a test tube or make gold from lead thunderstorm. As I stood at the door, I saw a stream of fire come from an old and beautiful oak in our yard. As soon as the dazzling light vanished, the oak had disappeared. I never saw anything so utterly destroyed.

At this time, a man who knew a lot about natural philosophy[3] was visiting us. Excited by what had happened, he began to explain his own ideas about electricity. Everything I had been studying grew suddenly uninteresting to me. I began to think that nothing would or could ever be known. I gave up the study of natural history. I immediately began to study mathematics. I thought that because mathematics could be proven, it alone was worthy of study.

When I look back, it seems to me that this sudden change of interest was my last chance to have a normal life. If I had continued to study mathematics, I would never have conducted the experiments that led to the tragedies of my life.

---

3. **natural philosophy** the equivalent of today's study of the natural sciences—chemistry, physics, and anatomy

2 Victor Continues His Education

When I was 17, my parents said that I should go to the University of Ingolstadt. My father thought that I should learn other customs than those of my native country. Before I could leave for Germany, however, the first great sorrow of my life occurred. Perhaps it was a hint of my future misery.

Elizabeth had caught scarlet fever. Her illness was severe, and she was in the greatest danger. My mother was able to nurse her back to health, but the result was fatal. On the third day my mother sickened, and she continued to get worse as time went by. On her deathbed, she joined my hands with Elizabeth's. Then she said, "My children, I have always hoped that you would someday marry. This hope for your marriage will now comfort your father. We shall all meet again in another world."

She died calmly, and her face showed affection even in death. I need not describe the grief we felt. Why should I describe a sorrow that all have felt and must feel? The time at length arrives when grief must give way to life. My mother was dead, but we still had duties to perform and lives to live.

The day of my departure for Ingolstadt finally arrived. Clerval spent the last evening with us. He had tried to persuade his father to let him study at Ingolstadt, too. However, his father could not be convinced. He was a narrow-minded trader who saw nothing but ruin in the hopes and ambitions of his son. Clerval, however, was committed not to be chained to the miserable details of business.

In the morning I went to the carriage that was to carry me away. They were all there. My father again blessed me, Clerval pressed my hand once more, and my Elizabeth gave me a kiss.

The journey to Ingolstadt was long and tiring. Finally, the high, white steeple of the town met my eyes. I was taken to my apartment to spend the evening as I pleased.

The next morning I delivered my letters of introduction and visited some of the professors. I first met M.[1] Krempe, professor of natural philosophy. He asked me questions about what I already knew. When I mentioned the authors I had read, he said, "Have you really spent your time on such nonsense? Every minute you wasted on those books is entirely lost. You have burdened your memory with useless names. In what desert land did you live? Was no one kind enough to tell you that these ideas are as musty as they are ancient? My dear sir, you must begin your studies anew."

So saying, he wrote a list of several books for me to read. M. Krempe was a little squat man, with a gruff voice and an ugly face. I didn't like him very much, so I wasn't eager to begin reading any of the books he recommended.

Before the first week had ended, however, I did meet a professor I liked. His name was M. Waldman. He was about 50 years old, with a friendly face. A few gray hairs covered his temples, but those at the back of his head were nearly black. His voice was the sweetest I had ever heard. His first lecture was about the

---

1. **M.** the abbreviation for the French title *Monsieur,* which means "Mister"

history of chemistry. He then talked about the present state of the science. He ended with words I will never forget.

He said, "The ancient teachers of this science promised the impossible and performed nothing. The modern masters promise very little. They know that metals cannot be changed and that life is a mystery. Even so, these modern scientists have indeed performed miracles. They have discovered how the blood circulates. They have learned the nature of the air we breathe. They have acquired new and almost unlimited powers. Who knows what future discoveries they might make?"

Such were the professor's words. As he spoke I felt as if my soul were fighting with an enemy. Soon my mind was filled with one thought, one idea, one purpose. So much has been done, exclaimed my soul. More, far more, will I achieve! I will pioneer a new way, explore unknown powers, and unfold to the world the deepest mysteries of creation.

I made up my mind to return to my ancient studies. I wanted to devote myself to a science for which I believed I had a natural talent. The next day I paid M. Waldman a visit. He was even more pleasant at home than he was in the lecture hall. I told him about my previous studies. When he heard the names Agrippa and Paracelsus, he smiled, but without the contempt M. Krempe had shown. He said, "Those men laid the foundations for modern science. Even though their work came to nothing, they were men of genius whose zeal can still inspire us."

I asked for his advice concerning the books I ought to read. M. Waldman said, "If you want to be a man of science, you must study every branch of natural philosophy, including mathematics." He then took me into his laboratory. He explained to me the uses of his various machines. He told me which ones I ought to buy for myself. He promised me the use of his own when I was advanced enough not to break them. He also gave me the list of books that I had requested. Thus ended a day I shall never forget. It decided my future.

From that day, natural philosophy, and particularly chemistry, became nearly my sole occupation. I read every book I could find on these subjects. I attended the lectures of, and became acquainted with, the men of science of the university. In M. Waldman I found a true friend and a fine teacher. In a thousand ways he made it easier for me to learn. He answered every question clearly, in a way that was easy to understand. I became such an eager student. The stars often disappeared in the light of morning while I was still working in my laboratory.

Two years passed in this way, during which I paid no visit to Geneva. I was busy, heart and soul, in the pursuit of some discoveries that I hoped to make. Only those who have experienced it can understand the fascination of science. In other studies, you go as far as those who have gone before you. There is nothing more to know. In science, however, there is continual food for discovery and wonder. At the end of two years, I had learned all that the professors at Ingolstadt could teach me. I thought of returning to my friends and my hometown. Then something happened that made me stay.

One of my favorite subjects was the structure of the human frame and, indeed, that of any living animal. What, I often asked myself, was the cause of life? It was a bold question, one that has ever been considered a mystery. To examine the causes of life, we must first study death. I began to study the science of anatomy, but this was not enough. I also studied the natural decay and breakdown of the human body upon death.

I had never been frightened by tales of supernatural horrors, superstition, and ghosts. A cemetery to me was just a place for bodies deprived of life, bodies that were now food for worms. Now I was led to examine the cause and progress of this decay. I spent days and nights in vaults and burial houses. I saw how the fine form of the human body was destroyed and wasted. I saw how the worm inherited the wonders of the eye and brain.

In the midst of this darkness, a sudden idea came to me. It was brilliant and wondrous, yet so simple. I became dizzy just thinking about what it meant. So many men of genius had studied the same science. I was surprised that I alone would discover so astonishing a secret.

Remember that I am not recording the vision of a madman. What I say is as true as the fact that the sun shines in the sky. After days and nights of incredible work, I discovered the cause of life. More than that, I became capable myself of giving life to lifeless matter.

I see by the look on your face, my friend, that you expect me to tell you this secret. That cannot be. Listen to my story and you will learn why I cannot tell you. Learn from me, if not by what I say, then at least by my example, how dangerous this secret is.

When I found this power placed in my hands, I thought a long time about the best way to use it. Although I could give life easily, preparing a frame for it—with all its fibers, muscles, and veins—was not so easy. I doubted at first whether I should try to create a being like myself, but I soon changed my mind. I knew I could succeed. I made up my mind to make a huge man, about eight feet tall and proportionately large.

I began to gather the parts I would need. My workshop was a solitary room at the top of the house. It was separated from all the other apartments by a staircase. I collected bones from burial houses. The dissecting room and the slaughterhouse also furnished many of my materials.

I worked all summer on this one pursuit. I forgot about everything else. I even neglected to write letters to my father, Elizabeth, and Clerval. I knew that my silence upset them, but I could not tear myself away from my work. I know now that human beings should never allow passion to disturb their peace. I do not think that the pursuit of knowledge is an exception to this rule. If your studies destroy your taste for simple pleasures and family affections, then those studies are wrong. If this rule were always followed, Greece would not have fallen, Caesar would have spared this country, and America would have been discovered more gradually.

But I will go on with my story. I continued to work. Another year passed, and I did not even notice the changing of the seasons. I was obsessed with my work. I shunned my fellow beings as if I had been guilty of a crime. Every day brought me closer to success. I promised myself that I would enjoy some exercise and amusement as soon as my creation was complete.

3 The Creature Comes to Life

It was on a dreary night of November that I saw the end of my work. I collected the instruments of life around me. Soon I would put the spark of being into the lifeless thing that lay at my feet. It was one in the morning, and the rain pattered against the window-panes. My candle was nearly burned out. By the glimmer of its faint light, I saw the dull, yellow eye of the creature open. It breathed hard, and its arms and legs began to move.

How can I describe my feelings at this moment? I had constructed his face to be beautiful. Beautiful? How could I have been so wrong? His yellow skin scarcely covered the muscles and veins. His hair was of a lustrous black and flowing. His teeth were pearly white. But his watery eyes seemed almost the same color as his shriveled skin. He had straight black lips. I had worked hard for almost two years for this. I had deprived myself of rest and health. Now that I had finished, the beauty of the dream vanished. Breathless horror and disgust filled my heart. I was unable to look at the being I had created. I rushed out of the laboratory and ran to my bedroom.

Unable to sleep I walked back and forth in my room. Finally, worn out, I threw myself on the bed in my clothes. I slept for a while. I dreamed that Elizabeth, young and healthy, was walking in the streets of Ingolstadt. Delighted and surprised I hugged her. As I kissed her, her face began to change. I thought I held the corpse of my dead mother in my

arms. I saw the worms crawling in the folds of the burial clothes.

I woke from my sleep in horror. Then by the dim and yellow light of the moon, I saw the miserable monster I had created. He held up the curtain that surrounded my bed. His eyes were staring at me. His jaws opened, and he muttered some sounds. He might have spoken, but I did not hear. I escaped and rushed down the stairs. I stayed in the courtyard for the rest of the night, walking back and forth.

No mortal can imagine the horror of that face. A mummy brought back to life could not be so hideous. I had looked at him while he was unfinished. He was ugly then. But when he started moving, he looked even worse.

In the morning I began to walk the streets. I was trying to avoid the wretch, whom I kept expecting to see. I did not dare return to my apartment. I walked in this way for some time, trying to calm down. Finally I came to the inn where carriages usually stopped. Here I halted, I knew not why. A coach from Switzerland drove up. As the door opened, Henry Clerval got out. He said, "My dear Frankenstein, I'm so glad to see you! How lucky that you should be here just as I arrived!"

Nothing could equal my delight on seeing Clerval. His presence brought back to my thoughts my father, Elizabeth, and all the scenes of home. In a moment I forgot my horror and misfortune. I felt suddenly, for the first time in many months, calm and serene joy. I welcomed my friend in the warmest manner, and we walked toward my college.

As we walked he told me how he had finally persuaded his father to let him go to college. He also told me how worried my father and Elizabeth had been.

Then he said, gazing full in my face, "I didn't notice at first how ill you appear. You are so thin and pale. You look as if you haven't been sleeping for several nights."

"You are right," I said. "I have not been resting, as you see. I hope, though, that my work has come to an end and that I am finally free." I could not tell him what had happened the night before. I then remembered that the creature might still be in my apartment. I dreaded seeing him, but even more, I dreaded that Clerval should see him.

I asked Clerval to wait at the bottom of the stairs, and I darted up to my room. I threw open the door, but nothing appeared. I stepped fearfully in and found the apartment empty. My bedroom was also freed of its hideous guest. I could hardly believe my luck. I clapped my hands for joy and ran down to Clerval.

We went up to my room, and the servant brought some breakfast. I was unable to remain for a single instant in the same place. I jumped over the chairs, clapped my hands, and laughed aloud. Clerval at first thought I was just glad to see him. When he observed me more closely, he saw a wildness in my eyes. My loud laughter began to frighten him.

"My dear Victor," he cried, "what is the matter with you?"

"Do not ask me," I shouted. I imagined that the monster came into the room and seized me. I struggled furiously and fell down in a fit. I did not recover my senses for a long, long time.

This was the beginning of an illness that kept me in bed for several months. During all this time, Clerval was my only nurse. Knowing how my father and Elizabeth would worry, he didn't tell them how ill I was. I kept imagining that I saw the monster, and I raved constantly about him. I'm sure that my words surprised Clerval.

Slowly I recovered. It was springtime when I came to my senses. "Dearest Clerval," I said, "how kind and good you are to me! This whole winter, instead of studying, you have been in this sickroom. How shall I ever repay you?"

"You will repay me by getting better. Now you are showing such improvement, you will perhaps be glad to read a letter. It has been sitting here for some days for you. It is from Elizabeth, I believe."

Clerval then put the following letter into my hands:

My dearest Victor,

You have been very ill, and even the letters of dear Henry are not enough to calm my fears. Henry says that you are forbidden to write, but just one word from you is all I need. I eagerly hope that you will soon be able to write.

Get well and return to us. You will find a happy, cheerful home and friends who love you dearly. Little change, except the growth of your two brothers, Ernest and William, has taken place since you left. Your little brother William is now five. I wish you could see him. He is tall for his age, with sweet, laughing blue eyes, dark eyelashes, and curling hair. When he smiles two little dimples appear on each cheek. He is rosy with health.

Since you left us, one change has taken place. Do you remember on what occasion Justine Moritz entered our family? Probably not, so I will refresh your memory. Her mother was a widow with four children. Justine was the third. She had always been a favorite of her father's, but her mother did not like her very much. After M. Moritz died, her mother treated

Justine badly. My aunt noticed this. When Justine was 12 years old, my aunt asked her mother if Justine could live with us as a servant.

A servant in Geneva does not mean the same as a servant in France and England. Justine was always treated with dignity. She was a great favorite of yours. I remember you once said that a glance from Justine could change a bad mood to a good one. My aunt was also fond of her, and she gave Justine a good education. Justine was very grateful, and you could see by her eyes that she almost adored my aunt.

When my dearest aunt died, everyone was too grief-stricken to notice poor Justine. Poor Justine was very ill, but other trials were ahead for her. One by one, her brothers and sister died. Except for Justine, her mother was left childless. The woman's conscience bothered her. She thought that her other children had died to punish her for having favorites. So a few months after you left, her mother called her back. Poor girl! She wept when she left our house. Not long after that, her mother died, too. Justine is now back with us, and we are so glad to have her.

Write soon, dearest Victor. One word will be a blessing to us.

Elizabeth Lavenza
Geneva, March 18, 17—

"Dear, dear Elizabeth!" I exclaimed when I had read her letter. I wrote immediately. Within two weeks I was well enough to leave my bedroom. The first thing I did was introduce Clerval to my professors. They had no way of knowing how much torture it was to hear them praise me. They thought it was because I was too modest. Little could they guess the real reason I disliked the entire subject of science.

Clerval had come to the university to study oriental languages. Together we studied Persian, Arabic, and Sanskrit. I felt a great relief to be away from the sciences. We spent the summer in these studies, and my return to Geneva was planned for the end of autumn. But one thing and another got in the way, including the snows of winter. The roads were blocked, and my journey was put off until the following spring. Clerval and I spent the winter cheerfully. When spring finally came, its beauty made up for its lateness.

May arrived, and I waited for a letter setting the date of my departure. While we waited, Clerval suggested a walking tour of the area. I was fond of exercise, and Clerval had always been my favorite companion on walks at home.

We spent two weeks walking about the countryside. My health and spirits became stronger with the fresh air I breathed. Clerval again taught me to love the beauty of nature and the cheerful faces of children. Excellent friend! How sincerely you loved me! I became the same happy creature who, a few years before, had no sorrow or care. A calm sky and green fields filled me with joy.

We returned to our college on a Sunday morning. The peasants were dancing. Everyone we met seemed happy. My own spirits were high, and I had feelings of great joy and happiness.

4 The Troubles Begin

On my return I found this letter from my father:

My dear Victor,

You have probably been waiting for a letter to fix the date of your return. I was at first tempted to write only a few lines to tell you when we would expect you. But that would be cruel, and I dare not do it. How would you feel if, instead of a happy welcome, you found only tears and misery? How can I tell you what has happened? How can I cause pain to my long absent son? I wish to prepare you for the sad news, but I know it is impossible. Even now your eye skims over the page to seek the words that will tell you the horrible story.

William is dead! That sweet child whose smiles warmed my heart! Victor, he has been murdered!

I will not try to console you. I will simply tell you what happened.

Last Thursday (May 7), Elizabeth, your two brothers, and I went for a long walk. The evening was warm and calm, and we walked farther than usual. It was already dusk when we started back. Then we discovered that William and Ernest, who had gone on ahead, were not to be found. We sat on a bench until they should return. Soon Ernest came and asked if we had seen his brother. He said that they had been playing hide and seek, but he could not find him.

We all searched for him until night fell. Then Elizabeth thought that he might have returned to the house. He was not there. We came back with torches and searched all night. About five in the morning I discovered my lovely boy stretched motionless on the grass. The print of the murderer's finger was on his neck.

When Elizabeth saw William's body, she examined his neck. Then she exclaimed, "O God! I have murdered my darling child!"

She fainted, and when she came to, she only wept and sighed. She told me that William had teased her to let him wear a very valuable miniature[1] of your mother. The miniature is gone, and it was probably this that tempted the murderer.

Come, dearest Victor. You alone can console Elizabeth. She weeps continually and blames herself for William's death. Come, Victor, but not with thoughts of revenge against the killer. Come with feelings of kindness and love for those who love you. Help us heal the wounds of our minds.

Your loving father,
Alphonse Frankenstein
Geneva, May 12, 17—

Clerval had been watching my face as I read this letter. I threw the letter on the table and covered my face with my hands.

"My dear Frankenstein," he exclaimed. "Are you always to be unhappy? My dear friend, what has happened?" I motioned for him to read the letter, while I paced back and forth. Tears also gushed from the eyes of Clerval as he read it.

"I cannot comfort you, my friend. What do you plan to do?" he said when he had finished.

---

1. **miniature** a very small portrait or other painting on ivory or metal, sometimes worn as jewelry

"To go instantly to Geneva. Come with me to order the horses." Soon I was on my sad way home. I had been away for almost six years. The closer I got to home, the more I felt my grief and fear. The gates of Geneva were closed when I got there. I had to spend the night in a nearby village. I couldn't sleep, so I decided to visit the spot where my poor William had been murdered. Unable to pass through the town, I had to cross the lake in a boat. During this short voyage, I watched as a storm approached. On landing I climbed a low hill so I could better watch the storm. Soon I felt the rain coming slowly in large drops. Then the violence of the storm quickly increased.

Vivid flashes of lightning lit up the lake, making it look like a vast sheet of fire. While I watched the tempest, I walked on with a hasty step. The war in the sky made my spirits rise. I clasped my hands and exclaimed aloud, "William, dear angel! This is thy funeral! This thy dirge!"

As I said this, I saw in the gloom a figure near a clump of trees. I could not be mistaken. A flash of lightning lit up the object. I could plainly see its huge size and its terrible ugliness. I knew it was the wretch to whom I had given life. What was he doing there? Could he be the murderer of my brother? No sooner did I think this than I knew it was true. No human being could have killed that child. *He* was the murderer! I could not doubt it. I thought of chasing him, but I knew I would never catch him.

No one could imagine the anguish I suffered that night, which I spent, cold and wet, in the open air. When day dawned, I went to my father's house. My first thought was to tell everyone what I knew. I quickly realized, however, that I would be seen as a madman.

I arrived at the house at five in the morning. I told the servants not to wake up the family and went into the library to wait. The first one to get up was Ernest, and he said, "Welcome, my dearest brother. I hope you will be able to comfort our father and Elizabeth! Poor William! He was our darling and our pride!"

Tears fell from my brother's eyes. He told me that the murderer had been discovered. He said it was Justine Moritz. The miniature had been discovered in one of her pockets.

I said, "You are wrong. I know who the murderer is." Just then, my father walked in. I saw unhappiness on his face, but he tried to welcome me cheerfully. Before he could say much, however, Ernest said, "Good God, Papa! Victor says that he knows who killed poor William."

"We do also, unfortunately," said my father.

"My dear father, you are wrong. Justine is innocent."

"If she is, God forbid that she should be found guilty. She is to be tried today. I sincerely hope that she will be found innocent."

This speech calmed me. I could not imagine that any circumstantial evidence could be strong enough to convict her. We were soon joined by Elizabeth. Time had changed her since I last saw her. She was even more beautiful than before. "Your arrival, dear Victor, fills me with hope," she said. "I am sure that Justine is innocent. We have lost not only that lovely, darling boy, but also this poor girl has been falsely accused. If she is condemned, I shall never know joy again. But I am sure she will be found innocent."

"She is innocent, my Elizabeth," I said. "That shall be proved. Fear nothing."

"How kind you are!" said Elizabeth. "Everyone else

thinks she is guilty, but I know that it is impossible."
She wept.

"Dearest Elizabeth," said my father. "Dry your
tears. If she is, as you believe, innocent, rely on the
justice of our laws."

We passed a few sad hours until eleven o'clock when
the trial began. Witnesses were called. Several strange
facts worked against her, which might have convinced
anyone who had no proof of her innocence, as I had.
She had been out the entire night of the murder.
Toward morning she had been seen by a market
woman. She was not far from the place where the body
of the murdered child had later been found. The market woman asked her what she was doing there.
Justine had answered in a confused way.

She returned to the house about eight o'clock.
When asked where she had passed the night, she said
that she had been looking for the child. When shown
the body, she fell into violent hysterics and kept to
her bed for several days. The miniature was then pro-
duced, which the servant had found in her pocket.
Elizabeth said it was the same one she had placed on
a ribbon around William's neck. A murmur of horror
filled the court.

Justine was called on for her defense. She said,
"God knows that I am innocent. I will explain the facts
that have been presented as evidence against me. I
hope my judges will interpret in my favor any circumstance that appears doubtful or suspicious." She then
said that she had spent the evening of the murder at
her aunt's house, about four miles from Geneva. On
her return at about nine o'clock, she met a man who
asked her if she had seen the lost child. She was surprised by what he said, and she spent several hours
looking for William.

By then, the gates of Geneva were shut, and she was forced to stay in a barn belonging to a cottage. She didn't want to wake the people who lived there, to whom she was well known. Most of the night she was awake. Toward morning she believed that she slept for a few minutes. Some steps disturbed her, and she awoke. It was dawn, and she left the barn to continue looking for William. The fact that she had seemed confused when questioned by the market woman was not surprising. After all, she had spent a sleepless night, and the fate of poor William was still unknown. She could not explain about the miniature.

"I know," she said, "how much this one circumstance goes against me. I cannot explain how it came to be in my pocket. I believe that I have no enemy on earth. No one could be so wicked as to destroy me on a whim. Did the murderer place it there? I know of no chance he might have had to do so. Then again why would he have stolen the miniature only to part with it so soon?

"I place my cause in the hands of my judges, and yet I see no room for hope. I beg to have some witnesses called who can speak about my character. If their words are not enough, then I must be condemned. Even so, I swear on my soul that I am innocent."

Several witnesses who had known Justine for many years came forward. They spoke well of her, but they were not enthusiastic enough. Perhaps they were frightened by the seriousness of the crime. Elizabeth saw that these witnesses were not going to be of much help to Justine. She asked permission to address the court.

"I lived with the child who was murdered," she said. "It may therefore be judged indecent of me to come forward on this occasion. Nevertheless, I must say what I know of Justine's character. I know the accused very well. I have lived in the same house with her. She was always the sweetest and most unselfish person. She cared for Madame Frankenstein in her last illness. Later, she took care of her own mother during a long illness. She was warmly attached to the child who is now dead. She acted toward him like a loving mother. I believe that she is completely innocent. She had no reason to do such a terrible thing. As for the miniature on which the chief proof rests, I would have given it to her if she wanted it."

The result of Elizabeth's testimony was not what she had hoped. The public turned even more strongly against Justine, accusing her of the worst ingratitude. I passed a night of terrible wretchedness. In the morning I went to the court. My lips and throat were parched. I dared not ask the fatal question. The officer knew who I was, and he told me what I wanted to know. The ballots had been thrown. They were all black, and Justine was condemned to death.

In the morning, Justine died by hanging. I observed the deep and voiceless grief of Elizabeth. I knew that her sorrow was my doing! I watched those I loved spend vain sorrow upon the graves of William and Justine. These innocent souls were the first victims of the monster I had created.

5 *Frankenstein Meets the Creature*

Even though I knew that the blood was flowing freely in my veins, I felt more dead than alive. A weight of despair and remorse pressed on my heart. Sleep fled from my eyes. I wandered like an evil spirit, for I had done something horrible in creating this monster. Yet my heart was filled with kindness and the love of virtue. I had begun life with good intentions. I had wanted to do something good for my fellow human beings. Now all was destroyed. No words can describe the torture and guilt I felt.

This state of mind preyed upon my health. I stayed away from people, wanting only to be alone. All sounds of joy were torture to me.

My father saw with pain how I had changed. He tried to get me to dispel the dark cloud that hung over me. "Do you think, Victor," said he, "that I do not suffer also? No one could love a child more than I loved your brother." (Tears came into his eyes as he spoke.) "But is it not our duty to help one another get on with life? It is also a duty owed to yourself. Too much sorrow makes a person unfit for society."

This advice, though good, did not apply to my case. My father could not know that terror was a part of my sorrow. I could only answer my father with a look of despair and try to hide myself from his view.

About this time we retired to our country house. This change was good for me. The shutting of the gates of Geneva each night at ten had been very annoying to me. Now I was free. Often after the family had retired for the night, I took the boat out. I would pass many hours upon the water. Sometimes with my sails set, I was carried by the wind. Other times after rowing into the middle of the lake, I simply drifted.

I was often tempted to plunge into the silent lake, let the waters close over me, and end my troubles forever. The only thing that stopped me was the thought of how much Elizabeth would suffer. I thought also of my father and my surviving brother. How could I leave them exposed and unprotected to the evil of the fiend whom I had set loose among them?

I lived in daily fear that the monster would appear again. I had a feeling that all was not over and that he would commit an even more terrible crime. There was always room for fear as long as anything I loved remained behind. When I thought of him, my hatred grew. I would have climbed the highest mountain if, when there, I could have thrown him to the base. I wished to see him again so that I could avenge the deaths of William and Justine.

Our house was a house of mourning. My father's health was deeply shaken. Elizabeth was sad and melancholy, unable to take any pleasure in life. She said, "I know that William was murdered, and I know that Justine was innocent. The murderer still walks about the world free and perhaps respected. I no longer see the world in the same way. I am beginning to think that there is no justice."

I listened to her words with extreme agony. I, not in deed but in effect, was the true murderer. Elizabeth saw the anguish in my face. She took my hand and said, "Dear Victor, the look on your face makes me tremble. Remember the friends around you. Have we lost the power to make you happy? Ah! While we love—while we are true to each other—what can disturb our peace?"

Not even Elizabeth could chase away the fiend that lurked in my heart. Nothing, it seemed, could save my soul from woe. I decided to leave my home for a while and seek comfort in the beauty of nature. I went to the valley of Chamounix.[1] I had visited it frequently during my boyhood. I hadn't been there for six years. *I* had changed drastically—but nothing in those savage and enduring scenes had changed.

I traveled on horseback and later by mule. The weather was fine. It was the middle of August, nearly two months after the death of Justine. The beauty of the mountains was breathtaking. The sound of the river raging among the rocks and the dashing of the waterfalls spoke of a mighty power. The winds whispered in soothing accents. However even this power and beauty could not make me forget my horror and despair.

At length I arrived at the village of Chamounix. I rented a room, and as soon as I placed my head upon the pillow, sleep crept over me.

I spent the following day roaming through the valley. Although the beautiful scenery did not remove my grief, it calmed me down a little. That night I slept well, and the next day I decided to climb the nearby mountain. I went without a guide for I was well acquainted with the path. Another person would only have destroyed the solitude I was seeking.

The mountain was steep, but the path was cut into short windings so that the climb was not too difficult. The biggest danger was that, in some places, the

---

1. **Chamounix** a valley in southeast France, northwest of Mont Blanc, the highest mountain in the Alps

slightest sound, such as speaking in a loud voice, could cause an avalanche.

It was nearly noon when I arrived at the top. I sat on a rock and gazed at the wonderful scene below me. My heart, which had been so sorrowful, now swelled with something like joy.

Just then I saw the figure of a man climbing toward me. He was moving with superhuman speed. He bounded over the ice where I had walked with such caution. His size seemed larger than that of a man. As he came closer, I saw that it was the wretch whom I had created. I trembled with rage and horror. He approached, his face expressing bitter anguish. His ugliness was almost too horrible for human eyes.

"Devil!" I exclaimed. "Do you dare approach me? Do you not fear my vengeance? Begone, vile insect, or rather stay, so that I may trample you to dust! If only that would restore the victims whom you have so wickedly murdered!"

"I expected such a welcome," said the creature. "Everyone hates the wretched, and I am the most wretched of all. Yet you are my creator. It is your fault that I am so wretched. You are bound to me until death. You want to kill me? How dare you sport thus with life? Do your duty to me and I will do mine to you. I have something to ask of you. If you do it, I will leave you and the world at peace. If you refuse, I will kill your remaining friends."

"Hated monster! Come closer so I may put out the spark of life I so foolishly gave you!"

"Be calm! I beg you to hear me out. Have I not suffered enough? Life, even though it is full of anguish, is dear to me, and I will defend it. Remember that you have made me stronger and taller than you. You wouldn't have a chance against me. However I have no wish to harm you. I am your creature, and you owe me something. Oh, Frankenstein, everywhere I see happiness that I alone cannot have. I was good, but misery made me a fiend. Make me happy, and I shall again be good."

"Begone! We are enemies, and I shall never do anything to help you!"

"How can I make you understand? You are my creator, and yet you hate me. What hope can I get from other people who owe me nothing? They reject and hate me. You are my only hope. Listen to my tale. Even the guilty are allowed to speak in their own defense before they are condemned. You accuse me of murder, and yet you would destroy your own creature.

"Hear my tale. It is long and strange. It is too cold for you out here, so let us go to the hut on the mountain. The sun is yet high in the heavens. Before it sets, you will have heard my story. Then it will be up to you. Either I will lead a harmless life away from people, or I will become the most dreaded enemy of your fellow creatures."

As he said this, he led the way across the ice. I followed. As I walked I weighed the various arguments he had used. I decided at least to listen to his tale. I was curious and at the same time compassionate. For the first time, I felt what the duties of a creator toward his creature were. I thought that I ought to help him be happy before I complained of his wickedness. Soon we entered the hut, the fiend with an air of joy, I with a heavy heart and sad spirits. But I agreed to listen. I sat by the fire that the creature had lighted. He thus began his tale.

6 The Creature's Story

"It is hard for me to remember the first days of my life. I could see, feel, hear, and smell, but I did not understand these sensations. Light bothered me, and I looked for shade. I found it in the forest near Ingolstadt. I rested there by a brook. I ate some berries, drank from the brook, and slept by the water.

"It was dark when I awoke. I felt cold and frightened. Before I had left your apartment, I covered myself with some clothes. But these were not enough to protect me from the dews of night. I was a poor, helpless, miserable wretch. I knew nothing. Feeling pain on all sides, I sat down and wept.

"Soon a gentle light stole over the heavens. I learned later that this was the moon. I gazed at it with wonder. I again went out to look for berries. I was still cold when under one of the trees I found a huge cloak. I covered myself with it and sat down on the ground. No ideas came to my mind. All was confused.

"Several days passed, and I began to sort out the sensations I was feeling. My vision became clearer. I began to realize that certain pleasant sounds came from the throats of the little winged animals I saw. Sometimes I tried to sing like the birds. The sounds that came from me frightened me into silence again.

"One day I found a fire that had been left by some wandering beggars. I was overcome with delight at its warmth. In my joy I thrust my hand into the live embers, but I quickly drew it out in pain. I found, with pleasure, that fire gave light as well as heat. I also found that the taste of certain foods was improved when placed on the live embers.

"Food, however, became scarce, and I was forced to leave the area and look elsewhere for food. I started to walk through the wood toward the setting sun. I walked for three days and at length came to open country. I saw a small hut, which was a new sight to me. Finding the door open, I entered. An old man sat there, near a fire, preparing his breakfast. Seeing me he shrieked loudly, left the hut, and ran across the fields. I greedily ate the rest of his breakfast. Then I lay down and fell asleep.

"It was noon when I awoke. I left the hut and continued across the fields. At sunset I arrived at a village, and I entered one of the cottages looking for food. The children inside shrieked. The whole village was stirred up, and the people chased me away, throwing rocks and other things at me.

"I escaped to the open country and fearfully took refuge in a low hovel.[1] It was joined to a cottage of neat and pleasant appearance. However, after my recent experience, I dared not enter it. The hovel was made of wood. It was so low that I could barely sit up in it. However, it was dry inside, and it protected me from the snow and rain. I was happy to have found a shelter against the weather and against the cruelty of people.

"This little shelter was a paradise compared to the forest, with its rain-dropping branches and cold ground. As I was counting my blessings, I heard a step. Looking through a small crack, I saw a young girl with a pail on her head passing before my hovel. Fifteen minutes later, she returned carrying the pail, which was now partly filled with milk.

---

1. **hovel** a small shed or shelter

"A young man met her. Both of them looked very sad. He took the pail and carried it to the cottage. She followed, and they went inside. The young man then left, carrying some tools. She kept busy, sometimes in the house and sometimes in the yard.

"I could see into the cottage through a small crack in the wall of my hovel. There was an old man inside, sitting in a corner near a small fire. Presently, the girl took an instrument from a drawer and gave it to the old man. He began to play, producing sounds sweeter than the voice of the thrush or the nightingale. They looked at each other with such kindness and affection that I felt strange sensations—a mixture of pain and pleasure. I stopped watching them, unable to bear these emotions.

"Soon after this, the young man returned, carrying a load of wood. The girl helped him with his burden, taking some of the wood into the cottage. She placed it on the fire. I watched as they prepared and ate their dinner. It was a simple one of bread, cheese, and soup. Then the old man walked outside for a few minutes, leaning on the arm of the youth. They all seemed to love each other very much, and yet the young man seemed extremely unhappy.

"When night came I was surprised to see that the cottagers had a way of keeping it light inside. They used candles, which I had never seen before. I was delighted to find that the setting of the sun did not put an end to the pleasure I had in watching them. The old man again played some music. Then the young man began to utter sounds I did not understand at all. I learned later that he was reading aloud, but at that time I knew nothing about words or letters.

"A short time later the family put out the lights and went to sleep. I lay on the floor of my hovel, but I could

not sleep. I thought about the people in the cottage. I longed to join them, but I dared not. I remembered how the villagers had treated me. I thought it best to remain hidden.

"The cottagers arose the next morning before the sun. They followed the same routine as they had the day before. I soon realized that the old man was blind. Nothing could exceed the love and respect that the younger cottagers showed toward him. They treated him gently and lovingly, and he smiled sweetly at them.

"They were not entirely happy. I began to think that if such lovely creatures were miserable, it wasn't so strange that I should be wretched. It took me a long time to figure out that one of the reasons for their unhappiness was their poverty. Their only food came from their own garden and the milk of their one cow. They were often hungry, especially the two younger ones. Several times they gave food to the old man when they had none for themselves.

"This kindness moved me. I had been stealing some of their food during the night for myself. When I saw that they had so little, I stopped. Instead, I gathered berries, nuts, and roots from a nearby wood.

"I found a way I could help them. I saw that the youth spent a lot of time collecting wood for the family fire. During the night, I often took his tools and brought home enough wood for several days. The first time I did this, I saw how surprised they were. I saw with pleasure that he did not go to the forest that day. Instead, he spent time repairing the cottage and working in the garden.

"I soon realized that they communicated with each other by making sounds. I strongly desired to learn how to do this. After several months, I learned and applied the words *fire, milk, bread,* and *wood.* I also learned the names of the cottagers themselves. The old man had only one name, *father.* The girl was called either *sister* or *Agatha.* The boy was called *Felix, brother,* or *son.* I learned several other words, but I did not yet understand them. They were *good, dearest,* and *unhappy.*

"I spent the winter in this way. I saw few human beings besides them. If any others happened to enter the cottage, their rude manners only made me realize how superior my friends were. I began to notice that Felix was the saddest of the group. He appeared to have suffered more deeply than the others.

"I could tell you many things that showed what kind of people they were. In the midst of poverty and want, Felix gave his sister the first little white flower that peeped out from beneath the snowy ground. Early in the morning, he cleared away the snow that blocked her path to the milk house. Then he brought in the wood that, to his surprise, he found replaced each day by an invisible hand. During the day, I believe he worked sometimes for a neighboring farmer. He would often leave, not returning until dinner. Yet he brought no wood back with him. He spent a lot of time reading to the old man and Agatha.

"This reading had me puzzled at first. Then I realized that when he read, he used many of the same sounds as when he talked. I figured out that he found on the paper signs for speech that he understood. I wanted to learn how to do this. It was impossible, however, because I didn't even understand the spoken language.

"I knew it was important to learn to speak. Only then would I be able to introduce myself to them. If I could speak, maybe I could get them to overlook the deformity of my figure. One day, I was terrified when I saw my reflection. At first I didn't believe it was I who was reflected in the pool of water. Then I became convinced that I was really the monster that I am. I was filled with the bitterest feelings of sadness. Alas! I did not yet entirely know the fatal effects of my appearance.

"As the sun grew warmer and the days longer, the snow vanished. I saw the bare trees and the black earth. Felix was very busy in the garden. Several new kinds of plants sprang up, which the family ate. These signs of comfort increased as the season advanced.

"My days followed a pattern. In the morning I watched the actions of the cottagers. When they were busy in the afternoon, I slept. The rest of the day I watched my friends. When they went to sleep, I went into the woods and collected my own food and wood for the cottage. Once or twice I heard them say *good spirit* or *wonderful* when they found the wood. However I did not understand those words then.

"I wanted nothing more than to find out why these creatures were so sad. I thought that I might be able to restore happiness to them. I looked upon them as superior beings. I imagined a thousand ways of presenting myself to them and how they would react to me. I imagined that they would be disgusted at first. But then, by my gentle nature, I would win their favor and later their love.

"These thoughts led me to try even harder to learn the art of language. I was learning to pronounce with some ease those words I understood.

"Spring was changing the earth. The birds sang in more cheerful notes, and the leaves began to bud on the trees. Happy, happy earth! My spirits were raised by the enchanting look of nature. The past was blotted from my memory. The present was tranquil, and the future full of hope.

7 The Creature Begins to Learn

"Spring advanced rapidly. The weather became fine and the skies cloudless. The beauty of the flowers and leaves surprised me. My senses were refreshed by a thousand scents of delight and a thousand sights of beauty.

"One day, someone tapped at the door of the cottage. It was a lady on horseback who had come with a guide. The lady was dressed in a dark suit and covered with a thick black veil. Agatha asked a question. The stranger answered, in a sweet accent, the name of Felix. Her voice was musical but unlike that of either of my friends. On hearing this word, Felix came up to the lady. When she saw him, she threw up her veil. I saw a face of angelic beauty. Her hair was shining black and braided. Her eyes were dark, but gentle and lively. Her skin was wondrously fair, each cheek tinged with a lovely pink.

"Felix seemed delighted to see her. Every trace of sorrow vanished from his face. His eyes sparkled, and his cheek flushed with pleasure., At that moment I thought him as beautiful as the stranger. She wiped a few tears from her lovely eyes. Then she held out her hand to Felix, who kissed it joyfully. He called her, as well as I could make out, his sweet Arabian.[1] She did not appear to understand him, but she smiled. He helped her off the horse, dismissed her guide, and brought her into the cottage. Felix spoke to his father,

---

1. **Arabian** a person from an Arab country

and the young stranger knelt at the old man's feet. She would have kissed his hand, but he raised her from her kneeling position and hugged her affectionately.

"I soon realized that the stranger neither understood nor was understood by the cottagers. She seemed to have a language of her own. They made many signs that I did not understand, but I saw that they were all happy to be together. Some hours passed, and I could see that she was trying to learn their language. The idea instantly occurred to me that I could learn at the same time. The stranger learned about 20 words at the first lesson. Most of them, indeed, were words that I already understood, but I learned a few new ones.

"As night came on, Agatha and the Arabian retired early. When they separated, Felix kissed her hand and said, 'Good night, sweet Safie.' He sat up much longer, talking with his father.

"The next morning Felix went out to his work, and Agatha did her usual morning routine. Then Safie, the Arabian, sat at the feet of the old man and played beautiful music on his guitar. She sang like a nightingale of the woods. When she finished, she gave the guitar to Agatha. Agatha played a simple air and sang along in sweet accents, but unlike the wondrous strain of the stranger.

"The days now passed as peaceably as before, except that joy had taken the place of sadness in the faces of my friends. Safie was always happy. She and I quickly learned the language. In two months I could understand almost everything they said. I may boast that I learned more quickly than she did. While I improved in speech, I also learned how to read, as it was taught to the stranger. This opened before me a wide field for wonder and delight.

"The book Felix read from was a history book. I therefore learned something about the manners, governments, and religions of the different nations of the earth. I learned about the great genius of the Greeks, of the wars and virtue of the early Romans, and of the decline of that mighty empire. I learned of chivalry, Christianity, and kings. I heard of the discovery of America. I wept with Safie over the fate of its original inhabitants.

"These stories inspired me with strange feelings. Were human beings at once so powerful, good, and magnificent, and yet also so vicious and base? For a long time I could not understand how anyone could murder another fellow being. I could not see why there were laws and governments. But when I heard details of vice and bloodshed, my wonder ceased. I turned away with disgust and loathing.

"As I listened to Felix's lessons, I realized that I had no place among human beings. I had no money, no friends, no kind of property. I was, besides, ugly and deformed. Was I then a monster, a blot upon the earth, from which all would flee?

"These thoughts brought me nothing but agony and sorrow. I learned that there was only one way to overcome the sensation of pain. That was death, a state that I feared yet did not understand. I was a miserable, unhappy wretch!

"Other lessons made even deeper impressions. I heard of the birth and growth of children and the love of the father and the mother for their child. I learned of the various relationships that bind one human being to another. But where were my friends and relations? I had no mother, no father, no brother, no sister. What was I? I could not answer this question.

"Still, the more I learned about the cottagers, the

more I loved them. The old man's name was De Lacey. He had come from a good family in France, where he had been wealthy, respected, and beloved. They had lived in Paris, surrounded by friends.

"The father of Safie had been the cause of their ruin. He was a Turkish merchant, and he had lived in Paris for many years. Then, for some reason that I could not learn, he got into trouble with the government. He was put into prison the very day that Safie came from Constantinople[2] to join him. He was tried and condemned to death. All of Paris was outraged at the injustice of his sentence. It was generally believed that his religion and wealth had been the cause of his condemnation.

"Felix had accidentally been present at the trial. When he heard the verdict, he vowed to help the man escape. During one of his visits to the man, when he told him of his plans, he met the man's daughter, Safie. Felix rejected the man's offers of money as a reward, but the man had noticed that Felix was interested in Safie. He offered the promise of her hand in marriage. Felix was too considerate of Safie's feelings to accept this offer, but he did hope to get to know her better.

"During the next few days, while Felix was preparing for the escape of the merchant, he received some letters from Safie. She told Felix that her mother was a Christian Arab, who was captured and made a slave by the Turks. Her great beauty won her the heart of Safie's father, who married her. Safie spoke of her mother in high and enthusiastic terms. She taught Safie about Christianity. She also taught her to aspire to higher powers of intellect and independence of spirit.

---

2. **Constantinople** an old name for the city of Istanbul in northwest Turkey

"This lady died, but her lessons were remembered by Safie, who did not want to return to Turkey with her father. The idea of marrying Felix and remaining in a country where women's rights were recognized was enchanting to her.

"Carrying out his plan, Felix helped Safie's father escape to Italy. Unfortunately, the French government quickly discovered what happened. De Lacey and Agatha were thrown into prison. Felix returned to France, hoping to free his father and sister by giving himself up. Instead, he was thrown into prison as well, and they remained there for five months until the trial. The result of the trial was that they were deprived of their fortune and exiled[3] from France.

"That is why they were living in the little cottage in Germany, where I found them. Felix soon found out that Safie's father had broken his promise. When he discovered that Felix no longer had money or rank, he changed his mind about allowing Safie to marry him. He decided to take her back to Constantinople, but he had to go first. His hiding place had been discovered by the French government, and he had to sail immediately. Safie was to stay in Italy with a trusted servant. She was to follow later with the greater part of his fortune, which was on its way.

"Safie found some papers belonging to her father. They told her where Felix was, and she quickly made her decision. Taking some jewels and money that belonged to her, she left Italy with a guide who understood her language. They set out for Germany, where Safie was finally reunited with Felix.

---

3. **exiled** sent from one's native land and forbidden to return; banished from one's own country

8 The Creature's Request

"Such was the history of my beloved cottagers. It impressed me deeply. As yet, I looked upon crime as a distant evil. Goodness and kindness were ever present before me. I longed to become an actor in the busy scene where such good qualities were displayed.

"One night, while I was in the forest collecting wood and food, I found on the ground a leather bag. Inside it were several pieces of clothing and some books. I brought the bag back to my hovel. Fortunately, the books were written in the same language I had been learning.

"I can hardly describe the effect these books had on me. As I read, I compared myself to the characters in the books. I found myself similar, yet at the same time strangely unlike these characters. I depended on nobody and I related to nobody. Who was I? What was I? Where had I come from? Where was I going? These questions continually came up, but I was unable to solve them.

"When I finished reading these books, I remembered some papers I had found earlier. They were in the pocket of the clothing I had taken from your laboratory. At first I had neglected them, but now that I was able to read, I began to study them carefully. It was your journal of the four months just before my creation. You described in these papers every step you took in your work.

"I am sure you remember these papers. Here they are. Every word in them tells about my accursed

50

beginning. All the details of those disgusting circumstances are given. I sickened as I read them. 'Hateful day when I received life!' I exclaimed in agony. 'Accursed creator! Why did you form a monster so hideous that even *you* turned from me in disgust? God, in pity, made humans beautiful, in his own image, but my form is a filthy copy of yours. Even Satan had his companions, fellow devils, to admire and encourage him, but I am alone and hated.'

"This is what I said when I was alone. Then when I thought about the goodness of the cottagers, I persuaded myself that they would welcome me. I believed that they would overlook my personal deformity. Could they turn from their door one, however monstrous, who wanted their compassion and friendship? I decided not to give up hope but to get myself ready for a meeting with them. This meeting would decide my fate. I put this off for a few months because I was afraid that I would fail. Besides, I found that I was learning so much each day. I thought that a few more months would make me much wiser.

"Several changes, in the meantime, took place in the cottage. The presence of Safie brought not only happiness but also greater material wealth than before. Felix and Agatha spent more time talking and having fun and were assisted in their work by servants. They did not appear rich, but they were happy and peaceful. I, on the other hand, became every day more upset. The more I learned, the more I could see what a wretched outcast I was. I had hope, it is true, but it vanished when I saw my reflection in water.

"I tried to put my fears aside, but it was difficult. I was alone. I remembered reading about Adam's prayers to his Creator. But where was mine? He had abandoned me. Bitterly, I cursed him.

"Summer changed to autumn, and autumn became winter. As I watched the cottagers, I saw that their happiness was not decreased by the absence of summer. They loved each other, and their joys were with each other. The more I saw of them, the more I wanted to claim their protection and kindness. My heart yearned to be known and loved by these friendly creatures.

"I was wise enough to realize that my ugliness was the chief object of horror with those who had seen me before. My voice, though harsh, was not terrible. I thought, therefore, that it would be best to speak to the old man first, when he was alone.

"One day, Safie, Agatha, and Felix went out for a walk. The old man, at his own desire, was left alone in the cottage. When his children had gone, he took up his guitar and played several sad but sweet airs. At first his face was lit up with pleasure, but as he continued, sadness came over him. At length, laying aside the instrument, he sat absorbed in thought.

"My heart beat quickly. This was the hour and moment of trial that would decide my hopes or realize my fears. The servants were gone to a neighboring fair. It was an excellent opportunity. I approached the door of the cottage and knocked.

" 'Who is there?' said the old man. 'Come in.'

"I entered. 'Pardon me for bothering you,' I said. 'I am a traveler in want of a little rest. I would appreciate it if you would let me sit before your fire.'

" 'Of course,' said De Lacey. 'Unfortunately, my children are not here. As I am blind, I am afraid I cannot get any food for you.'

" 'Do not trouble yourself, my kind host. I have food. It is warmth and rest only that I need.'

" 'You speak French,' said the old man. 'Are you French?'

" 'No,' I said, 'but I was educated by a French family. I am now going to claim the protection of some friends, whom I dearly love. These people have never seen me. In fact, I have no relation or friend on earth. I am full of fears, for if I fail there, I am an outcast in the world forever.'

" 'Where do these friends live?'

" 'Near this spot.'

" 'Tell me your story. Perhaps I can help you. I am blind and cannot judge your face, but something in your words tells me that you are sincere.'

" 'Excellent man! I thank you. From your lips first have I heard the voice of kindness directed toward me. Your kindness assures me of success with those friends I am about to meet.'

" 'Who are these friends?'

"I paused. This was the moment of decision. Just then I heard the steps of the young people. I had not a moment to lose. I seized the hand of the old man and cried, 'Now is the time! Save and protect me! You and your family are the friends I seek!'

" 'Great God!' exclaimed the old man. 'Who are you?'

"At that instant the cottage door was opened, and Felix, Safie, and Agatha entered. Who can describe the horror on their faces? Agatha fainted, and Safie ran out of the cottage. Felix began to strike me violently with a stick. I could have torn him limb from limb, but I did not. Overcome by pain and anguish, I ran from the cottage and escaped to the woods.

"What a miserable night I passed! Not a single person existed who would pity or help me. Should I feel kindness toward my enemies? No! From that moment

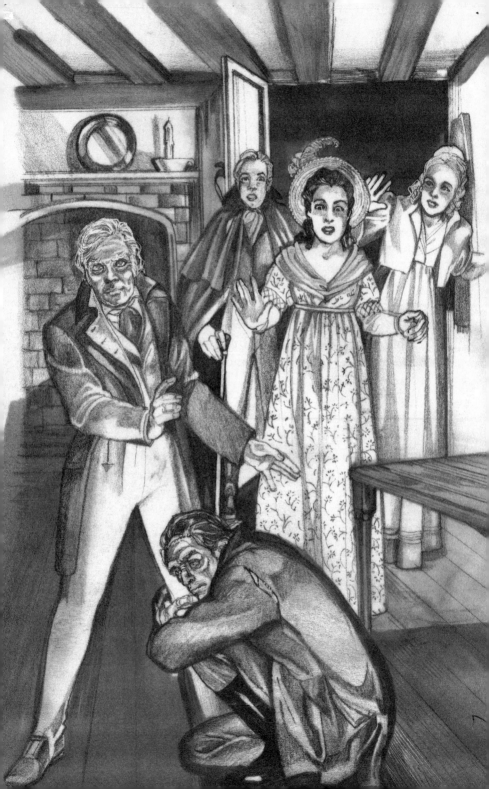

I declared everlasting war against the species and, more than all, against you. I had learned from your papers that your home was in Geneva. Toward this place I directed my steps.

"Geography was among the lessons that Felix had taught Safie. I knew, therefore, that Geneva was southwest of where I was. I used the sun as my only guide, for I could not ask directions from a single human being. My travels were long and my sufferings intense. I could travel only at night, and I found no shelter. The closer I got to Geneva, the more deeply I felt the spirit of revenge in my heart.

"One incident happened along the way that made me even angrier. Spring was beginning to warm the earth. One morning, it was so beautiful that I decided to continue my journey even after the sun had risen. The loveliness of the sunshine cheered me, reviving long-dead emotions of gentleness and pleasure. "Suddenly I heard the sound of voices, so I hid myself behind a tree. A young girl came running toward the spot where I was hidden. She was laughing, as if she ran from someone in sport. She continued along the steep sides of the river when her foot slipped and she fell into the rapid stream. I rushed into the river and saved her. Suddenly a man approached, probably the person from whom she had playfully fled. On seeing me, he ran toward me, tore the girl from my arms, and ran toward the woods. Then he turned around, aimed a gun at me, and fired. I sank to the ground, and the man escaped into the woods.

"This, then, was my reward for saving a human life! Inflamed by pain, I vowed eternal hatred and vengeance to all humankind. It took several weeks for my wound to heal, and then I continued my journey. I reached Geneva two months later.

"It was evening when I arrived, and I hid in the fields surrounding the city. I began to plan how I would approach you. Just then, a beautiful child came running nearby, with all the joy of childhood. Suddenly, as I gazed on him, an idea came to me. This little creature had no prejudices. He was too young to have developed a horror of deformity. If, therefore, I could seize him and educate him as my companion and friend, I would not feel so alone.

"So I seized the boy as he passed and drew him toward me. As soon as he saw me, he screamed. I said, 'Child, what is the meaning of this? I will not hurt you. Listen to me.'

"He struggled violently. 'Let me go, monster! Ugly wretch! You wish to eat me and tear me to pieces. Let me go or I will tell my papa.'

" 'Boy, you will never see your father again. You must come with me.'

" 'Hideous monster! Let me go. My papa is M. Frankenstein. He will punish you.'

" 'Frankenstein! You belong then to my enemy! You shall be my first victim!'

"The child still struggled and screamed. I grasped his throat to silence him. In a moment he lay dead at my feet.

"I gazed at my victim, and my heart filled with triumph. This will indeed cause my enemy great misery! I thought.

"As I looked at the child, I saw something glittering from a ribbon around his neck. It was a portrait of a most lovely woman. For a few moments I gazed with delight on her beauty, but soon my rage returned. I remembered that I was forever deprived of the delights that such beautiful creatures could bring.

"Then I left the spot where I had committed the murder. Looking for a hiding place, I entered a barn that I thought was empty. When I got inside, I saw a young woman sleeping on some straw. She was not as beautiful as the one whose portrait I held, but she was blooming in the loveliness of youth and health. Here, I thought, is one of those who would smile on all but me. I bent over her and whispered, "Awake, fairest, your lover is near—he who would give his life for just one friendly smile from you. My beloved, awake!'

"The sleeper stirred. A thrill of terror ran through me. Would she awake, see me, curse me, and reveal me as the murderer? Surely she would do so, if her eyes opened and she saw me. Then I thought, Not I, but she shall suffer. She shall be blamed for the murder I committed. Thanks to the lessons of Felix, I knew something about the law and how it worked. I bent over her and placed the portrait securely in one of the folds of her dress. She moved again, and I fled.

"For some days I stayed near this place. At times I wished to see you. At other times I made up my mind to quit the world and its miseries forever. At length I wandered toward these mountains, consumed by a burning passion that you alone can fulfill. We may not part until you have promised to grant my request. I am alone and miserable. No person will associate with me. One as deformed and horrible as I am would not deny herself to me. My companion must be like me, with the same defects. This being you must create."

9 Victor Postpones the Wedding

The being finished speaking and looked at me, expecting a reply. But I was bewildered, confused, and unable to understand the full extent of his request. He continued, "You must create a female for me. This you alone can do, and I demand it of you as a right. You must not refuse."

The last part of his story had increased the anger that had died away while he spoke of his peaceful life among the cottagers. I could no longer control my rage. "I do refuse it," I replied. "No torture shall ever make me consent. Shall I create another like you? Together, your wickedness could destroy the world! Begone! I have answered you. The answer is no!"

"You are wrong," replied the fiend. "I will tell you why. I am evil because I am miserable. Am I not hated by everyone? Even you, who created me, would be glad to tear me to pieces. You would not call it murder to kill me, the work of your own hands. If I cannot inspire love, I will cause fear. I consider you my archenemy because you are my creator. To you I swear undying hatred. I will do my best to destroy you. I will not finish until I ruin your happiness completely, so that you shall curse the hour of your birth."

His anger contorted his face, but finally he calmed himself and went on. "I wanted to reason with you. If any human being were kind to me, I would return the kindness a thousand times. For that one person's sake, I would make peace with all of humankind! But I know that nobody will ever be kind to me. What I ask of you is reasonable. I demand a creature of another sex but as hideous as myself. It is true that we both shall be monsters, cut off from all the world. But that will make us more attached to each other. Our lives will not be happy, but they will be harmless. Oh! My creator, make me happy. Let me feel gratitude toward you. Do not deny this request!"

I was moved. I shuddered when I thought what might happen if I did this, but I understood his request. His story showed that he had feelings. Did I not, as his maker, owe him whatever happiness I could grant? He continued speaking.

"If you consent, neither you nor any other human being will ever see us again. We will go to the vast wilds of South America. We will sleep outdoors and eat acorns and berries. We will be at peace, and we will bother nobody. I now see compassion in your eyes. Let me seize this moment and persuade you to promise what I so strongly desire."

"You say you will live in the wild, where the beasts of the field will be your only companions. How can you, who long for the love of humanity, promise this? You will return, and you will again seek human kindness. You will again meet rejection, and your evil passions will be renewed. Then you will have a companion to aid you in the task of destruction. This may not be. Stop talking about it, for I cannot do it."

"I swear that this will not happen. My life will pass in peace, and in my dying moments, I shall not curse my maker."

His words had a strange effect on me. I began to think that I had no right to keep from him the happiness that was yet in my power to give. "You swear," I said, "to be harmless. How can I trust you?"

"If I have no ties and no affections, I will only feel

hatred. If, on the other hand, I have love and affection, I will become one with the chain of existence from which I am now excluded. I would have no reason to harm anyone."

I thought about what he said. His power and threats were part of what I thought about. He could do a lot of damage if I refused his request. I said, "I will do what you ask if you promise to leave Europe forever. You must also leave every other place where people live as soon as I shall give you a female who will go with you into exile."

"I swear," he cried, "that if you grant my request, you shall never see me again. Go to your home, and begin your work. I shall watch you. When you are almost finished, I shall appear." Saying this, he suddenly left, fearful, perhaps, that I would change my mind. I saw him descend the mountain faster than the flight of an eagle.

His story had taken the whole day. The sun was setting when he left. It took me a long time to descend the mountain. It was morning before I got to Chamounix. I didn't stay there but returned immediately to Geneva. My family was alarmed at my wild appearance, but I answered no questions. Yet I loved them deeply. To save them from the monster, I decided to get started on my terrible task right away.

Still I could not begin. Weeks passed. I spent whole days on the lake alone in a little boat, thinking about how to proceed. I had heard of some scientific discoveries in England that might help, but I did not want to go there.

One day, my father said, "You seem so unhappy. For some time, I could not figure out the reason, but yesterday an idea struck me. You know that I have always looked forward to your marriage with our dear

Elizabeth. You have been attached to each other since childhood. You appear entirely suited to each other. But perhaps she seems more like a sister than a wife. Perhaps you have even met someone else you would rather marry but feel that you are bound in honor to Elizabeth. Maybe this is why you are in such misery."

"My dear father, believe me when I say that I love Elizabeth deeply. My only hope for future happiness lies in our marriage."

"I am glad to hear that, Victor," said my father. "But the gloom that seems to have taken hold of your mind has me worried. Tell me, therefore, if you object to getting married right away. But do not think that a delay on your part would cause me any serious problems. All I want is your happiness. I need to hear from you what you want to do."

I thought about what my father said. Alas! The idea of an immediate marriage was one of horror and dismay. I was bound by a promise that I had not yet fulfilled and dared not break. If I broke my promise, what miseries would come to my family? Could I marry with this deadly weight yet hanging around my neck? I must do what I had promised and let the monster depart with his mate. Only then could Elizabeth and I be married.

I told my father, therefore, that I needed to visit England. I did not tell him why. He was glad to find that I was able to take pleasure in the idea of such a trip. He hoped that the change of scene would do me some good. The length of my stay was left to my own choice. A few months, or at most a year, was the period we agreed on. Without asking me, however, he and Elizabeth arranged that Clerval should go with me. At first, I was upset that I would not be alone, but then I was glad to have the company. Clerval might even stand between me and my enemy. If I were alone, wouldn't the creature force his hated presence on me?

To England, therefore, I went. It was understood that I would marry Elizabeth as soon as I returned. I knew that my family would be safe from the creature, for he had told me he would be watching me. I left Geneva toward the end of September. During the entire journey, all I could think of was the work I had to do when I got to England.

Clerval met me along the way. How great was the contrast between us! He was alive to every new scene, joyful at the beauty of the setting sun, and happy when he saw it rise. I, on the other hand, was a miserable wretch, haunted by a curse that shut up every avenue to enjoyment.

The countryside through which we traveled was beautiful, but I couldn't enjoy it. Clerval! Beloved friend! Even now it delights me to remember how you enjoyed the beauty of nature as we traveled. Where does he now exist? Is this gentle and lovely being lost forever? Does his mind exist now only in my memory? No, it is not so. Your body may be decayed, but your spirit still visits and consoles your unhappy friend.

Pardon this gush of sorrow. These words are but a slight tribute to the worth of Clerval. I will continue my story.

We traveled through Holland, and from there we went by sea to England. It was on a clear morning, in the latter days of December, that I first saw the white cliffs of Britain. Finally, we saw the numerous steeples of London.

10 Victor Makes a Decision

We stayed in London for several months. I spoke to the scientists who had information that could help me. Clerval kept himself busy with other interests. In Clerval, I saw the image of my former self. He was interested in the life around him, and he was eager to have new experiences.

He was also pursuing a goal he had in mind. His plan was to visit India, believing that he could help in the progress of European colonization and trade. In England, he could move toward this goal.[1] He was always busy, and the only thing that stood in the way of his enjoyment was my sorrowful mind.

I tried to hide my sadness from him as much as possible. I often refused to go out with him, claiming I was too busy, so that I could remain alone. I now also began to collect the materials I needed for my new creation. This was like the torture of single drops of water continually falling on the head.

After passing some months in London, we received a letter from a person in Scotland. He had visited us in Geneva once. He invited us to visit him in Perth.[2] Clerval wanted to go, and so I agreed.

We had arrived in England in October, and it was now February. We decided to go to Perth by the end of March and return to London about the end of July. I packed up my chemical instruments and the materials

---

1. At this time, England had strong political ties with India.
2. **Perth** a city in Scotland

I had collected. I decided to finish my work in some hidden spot in the Scottish highlands.

I enjoyed the scenery we saw along the way, but my enjoyment was embittered by sad memories. When I was young, the sight of beauty in nature could always interest my heart. But I was now a blasted tree. A lightning bolt had entered my soul, and I felt like a miserable spectacle of wrecked humanity.

Sometimes I thought that the fiend was following me and might murder my companion. When these thoughts came over me, I would not leave Clerval for a moment. Instead, I would follow him like a shadow to protect him from the monster.

We finally arrived in Perth, where our friend expected us. But I was in no mood to laugh and talk with strangers. So I told Clerval that I wished to tour Scotland alone. "Go ahead," I said, "and enjoy yourself here in Perth. Let's meet back here in about a month." When Clerval saw that I meant this, he stopped trying to talk me out of it. "I would rather go with you, but I know you want to go alone. Hurry back. I'll look forward to your return."

Having parted from my friend, I went to a remote spot of Scotland to finish my work alone. I did not doubt that the monster followed me. I felt that he would show himself when I was finished so that he might receive his companion. I found a place on a remote island where I could work. This island was hardly more than a rock. The soil was barren, with barely enough pasture for a few miserable cows. Only five people lived on the island, and they were thin and gaunt. Vegetables and bread, which they considered luxuries, came from the mainland about five miles away.

On the whole island, there were but three miserable

huts. One of these was vacant when I arrived, so I rented it. It had only two rooms. The roof was falling, the walls were not plastered, and the door was off its hinges. I ordered the necessary repairs, bought some furniture, and took possession.

Here, I worked every morning. In the evening, I walked on the stony beach of the sea, listening to the waves as they roared and dashed at my feet. It was a monotonous yet ever-changing scene.

As my work continued, it became every day more horrible to me. Sometimes I could hardly enter my laboratory for several days. Other times, I labored day and night in order to complete my work. It was indeed a filthy process. My heart often sickened at the work I was doing.

I began to grow restless and nervous. Every moment I feared to meet the monster. Sometimes I sat staring at the ground, afraid to look up. I feared to leave the sight of my fellow beings, for when I was alone he might come to claim his companion.

Meanwhile, I worked on, and my labor was already considerably advanced. I looked toward its completion with a fearful yet eager hope. My hope, however, was mixed with strange forebodings of evil. These forebodings made my heart sicken.

I sat one evening in my laboratory. The sun had set, and the moon was just rising from the sea. I did not have enough light for my work, so I sat idle. As I sat, I thought about what I was doing. Three years before, I was doing the same kind of work. I had created a fiend that had brought great sorrow to my heart.

I was now about to form another being who might turn out even worse. He had sworn to leave the neighborhood of humanity and hide himself in the wilderness, but she had not. Suppose she refused to go along with an agreement made before her creation? They might also hate each other. She could turn from him in disgust, and he would become more angry.

If they left Europe and went to the deserts of the new world, they might produce children. A race of monsters would be set upon the earth, making human life full of terror. Did I have a right to inflict this curse upon coming generations? I had been struck senseless by his terrible threats. Now for the first time, I began to think that future ages might curse me for what I was about to do.

I trembled, and my heart failed within me. Then, looking up, I saw him by the light of the moon. He was standing by the window. A ghastly grin wrinkled his lips as he gazed on me. Yes, he had followed me in my travels. Now he had come to check my progress and to claim his mate.

As I looked at him, his face expressed great evil and treachery. I thought with a sensation of madness on my promise. Then trembling with passion, I tore to pieces the thing on which I was working. The wretch saw me destroy the creature on whose future he depended for happiness. With a howl of despair and revenge, he ran away.

Some time later, he returned. I heard the sound of his footsteps approaching the hut. The door opened, and he walked in. He said, "You have destroyed the work you began. Do you dare to break your promise? Do you dare to destroy my hopes?"

"Begone! I do break my promise. I will never create another like you!"

"You think you are miserable now! I can make you so wretched that you will hate the light of day. You are my creator, but I am your master! Obey!"

"Your threats cannot make me do an act of evil. I am firm. Your words will not change my mind!"

The monster saw that I was determined. "Shall each man," he cried, "find a wife, and each beast have a mate, and I be alone? I had feelings of affection, and they were met by hate. Beware! You can blast my other passions, but revenge remains. I may die, but first you shall curse the sun that gazes on your misery. Beware, for I am fearless and therefore powerful. You will be sorry for this!"

"I am no coward! I will not bend before your words," I cried. "Leave me. I will not change my mind!"

"It is well. I shall go. But remember that I shall be with you on your wedding night."

I would have seized him, but he ran away. In a few minutes I saw him leaving in a boat, which shot across the waters with an arrowy swiftness. All was again silent, but his words rang in my ears. *"I shall be with you on your wedding night."* That then was the hour I would die. I was not afraid of this, but when I thought of Elizabeth's sorrow, tears streamed from my eyes. I resolved not to fall before my enemy without a bitter struggle.

The night passed away. In the morning, I took a walk on the beach. At about noon, I lay down on the grass and was overpowered by a deep sleep. When I awoke, I felt refreshed, and I began to think about what had happened the night before. It seemed like a dream, yet it was as clear as reality.

I sat on the shore for the rest of the afternoon. That evening, a fishing boat landed close to me, and one of the men brought me a packet. It contained letters from Geneva and one from Clerval. He asked me to join him. He said that he was getting ready to go to India, and he wished to spend some time with me before he left. He asked me, therefore, to leave my solitary island and to meet him at Perth. This letter called me back to life, and I decided to leave the island within two days.

Before I left, there was a task to perform. I had to get rid of the remains of the half-finished creature. I decided to take them out to sea and dispose of them in the ocean. I went to my laboratory and put all the pieces into a basket, with a great quantity of stones.

Between two and three in the morning the moon rose. Putting my basket into a little boat, I sailed out about four miles from the shore. The scene was perfectly solitary. A few boats were returning to land, but I sailed away from them. I felt as if I was about to commit a dreadful crime. At one time the moon, which had before been clear, was suddenly covered by a thick cloud. I took advantage of the moment of darkness to cast my basket into the sea. I listened to the gurgling sound as it sank, and then I sailed away from the spot.

The air was pure, and it refreshed me and filled me with pleasant sensations. I decided to stay out on the water for a while. Fixing the rudder in a direct position, I stretched myself at the bottom of the boat. Clouds hid the moon, and I heard only the sound of the boat. The murmur lulled me, and in a short time I slept soundly.

It was daylight when I awoke. I had drifted far from the coast. The wind was high, and I found that I could not sail in the right direction. I confess that I felt a few sensations of terror. I had no compass, and I did not know much about this part of the world. I might be driven out into the open sea. I was hungry and thirsty, and I thought I might die out there. I thought of Elizabeth, of my father, and of Clerval. When I thought how the monster might hurt them, I almost despaired.

Some hours passed, and the wind died away to a gentle breeze. The sea became free of breakers. Suddenly I saw a line of high land toward the south. I used part of my clothing to construct an additional sail. I steered my course toward the land, and I was finally able to find a harbor. I entered it, my heart bounding with joy.

As I was docking, several people crowded around me. They seemed surprised to see me, but instead of helping me, they spoke sharply to me. As soon as I got out of the boat, one of them told me to follow him to Mr. Kirwin's, "to give an account of yourself."

"Who is Mr. Kirwin? Why should I give an account of myself? Is this not a free country?" I asked.

"Ay, sir, it is free enough to honest folks. Mr. Kirwin is our local judge. You are to give an account of the death of a gentleman who was found murdered here last night."

This answer startled me. But I presently recovered myself. I was innocent. That could easily be proved. So I followed the crowd in silence to one of the best houses in the town. Little did I then expect the sorrow that was in a few moments to overwhelm me. This sorrow would put an end to any fear I ever had of shame or death.

I must stop here. It requires all my strength to recall the events that I am about to relate.

11 Clerval's Fate

I was brought to the judge, an old, good man with calm and mild manners. He gave me, however, a stern look. Then turning toward the others, he asked who appeared as witnesses on this occasion.

About half a dozen men came forward. One was selected by the judge. He stated that he had been out fishing the night before with his son and brother-in-law, Daniel Nugent. At about ten o'clock, they saw a strong northerly wind rising, so they put in for port. It was a very dark night, as the moon had not yet risen. Instead of landing at the harbor, they put in at a creek about two miles below. He walked on first, carrying some of the fishing tackle, and his companions followed.

As he was walking along the sands, he struck his foot against something and fell to the ground. His companions came up to assist him. By the light of their lantern, they found that he had fallen on the body of a man who was to all appearance dead. Their first thought was that he had drowned and had been thrown on shore by the waves. Then they found that his clothes were not wet, and even that the body was not then cold.

They instantly carried the body to a nearby cottage and tried to restore it to life, but in vain. It appeared to be a handsome young man, about 25 years old. He had apparently been strangled. The only sign of violence was the black mark of fingers on his neck.

The first part of this statement did not in the least interest me. But when the mark of the fingers was mentioned, I remembered the murder of my brother. I became extremely upset, my limbs trembled, and a mist came over my eyes. I had to lean on a chair for support. The judge observed me closely and of course grew suspicious.

The son said the same thing as his father. Then Daniel Nugent took the stand. He swore that, just before the fall of his companion, he saw a boat with a single man in it, not far from the shore. As far as he could see by the light of a few stars, it was the same boat in which I had just landed.

One woman confirmed that a boat with one man in it pushed off from the same part of the shore where the body was later found. Another woman confirmed that when the body was brought to her cottage, it was not cold.

Several other men took the stand. They agreed that, because of the strong wind, it was very probable that I had been beaten about for many hours. They also agreed that I had been forced to return nearly to the same spot from which I had left.

Mr. Kirwin, on hearing this evidence, had me taken to the room where the body lay. He wanted to see what effect the sight of it would have on me.

How can I describe my feelings? I cannot think about that terrible moment without shuddering and agony. When I saw the lifeless form of Henry Clerval stretched before me, I gasped for breath. Throwing myself on the body, I cried, "Have you also, my dearest Henry, been destroyed by my hand? Two I have already destroyed. Other victims await their destiny. But you, Clerval, my friend—"

I was carried out of the room in strong convulsions.[1] I soon developed a high fever. I lay for two months on the point of death. My ravings, as I later heard, were frightful. I called myself the murderer of William, of Justine, and of Clerval. Sometimes I begged for help in destroying the fiend who tormented me. I screamed with agony and terror. Because I spoke French, only Mr. Kirwin understood me. But my gestures and cries frightened everyone else in the prison to which I was brought.

One day, while I was slowly recovering, Mr. Kirwin entered my prison cell. He asked if he could do anything to make me more comfortable. He told me he was sympathetic to my case. He was sure evidence would be found to free me from the criminal charge.

"That is my least concern," I replied. "I am the most miserable of mortals. Tortured as I have been, can death be any evil to me?"

"Nothing indeed could be more agonizing than what you have been through. You were thrown, by some surprising accident, on this shore, seized immediately, and charged with murder. The first sight presented to you was the body of your friend, murdered and placed, as it were, by some fiend across your path."

I was surprised at the knowledge he seemed to have about me. He explained that he had read all the papers that had been found in my pockets. He had found a letter from my father. He instantly wrote to Geneva to tell my family about my misfortune and illness. In fact, he said that my father had come to visit and was now waiting to see me.

Nothing could have given me greater pleasure than

---

1. **convulsions** uncontrolled muscle contractions

the arrival of my father. I asked, "Are you then safe—
and Elizabeth—and Ernest?"

My father calmed me by saying that everyone was
safe. We were not allowed to visit for very long, for my
health was still in question. But over the next month, I
gradually got better. The appearance of my father was
to me like that of my good angel.

After three months in prison, I was finally brought
to trial. Evidence was brought forth proving that I was
on the Orkney Islands in Scotland at the hour the body
of my friend was found on the coast of Ireland. I was
immediately freed from prison. My father joyfully
arranged for our journey home to Geneva. I did not
share my father's joy, for to me the walls of a dungeon
or a palace were alike hateful. The cup of life was poi-
soned forever. Yet one duty remained to me. That was
to watch over the lives of those I loved and to lie in
wait for the murderer.

The voyage from Ireland to France came to an end,
and my father and I proceeded to Paris. We decided to
stay there and rest before continuing on to Geneva,
for I had overtaxed my strength. A few days before we
were to leave Paris, I received the following letter from
Elizabeth:

My dear Victor,

I am so happy that you are on your way home. My
poor dear, how you must have suffered! Yet I hope to
find that your heart is not totally void of comfort and
peace. Before I see you, however, I feel that some
things need to be said. I dare not postpone this any
longer. I have often wished to express this to you, but I
have never had the courage to begin.

You well know, Victor, that our marriage has been

the dream of your parents ever since we were children. We were loving playmates during childhood and, I believe, dear and valued friends to each other as we grew older. But as brother and sister often feel affection toward each other, without wanting a closer union, may this also be our case? Tell me the truth, Victor. Do you love another?

You have traveled, and you have spent several years of your life at Ingolstadt. I will understand if you regret our engagement. I confess to you that I love you, and all my dreams of the future have you in them. But I desire your happiness as well as my own. If you are planning to go through with this marriage merely to honor your parents' wishes, please do not. My only wish is to see you happy.

Do not let this letter disturb you. You don't have to answer it until you get here, if it will give you pain. If I see but one smile on your face when we meet, I shall need no other happiness.

Elizabeth Lavenza
Geneva, May 18, 17—

This letter made me remember the fiend's threat— *"I shall be with you on your wedding night."* I remembered that on that night he would do whatever he could to destroy me. On that night he had promised to complete his crimes by my death.

Well, be it so. A deadly struggle would take place. If he won, I would be at peace, and his power over me would be ended. If I won, I would be a free man. Alas! What freedom? I would always be haunted by the deaths of William, Justine, and Clerval. But in my Elizabeth, I possessed a treasure that would balance the horrors of the remorse and guilt I would forever carry.

Sweet and beloved Elizabeth! I read her letter again and again. I thought about whether my marriage would hasten my fate. My death might indeed happen a few months sooner. But if he suspected that I postponed the marriage because of his threat, he would surely find other, perhaps more dreadful, means of revenge.

In this state of mind I wrote to Elizabeth. I told her that my only hopes for happiness were centered on our marriage. I also wrote, "I have one dreadful secret to tell you. I will tell you this tale of misery and terror the day after our marriage. Until then, do not mention it, I beg you."

We were in Geneva about a week later. Sweet Elizabeth welcomed me with warm affection, and yet tears were in her eyes as she saw how ill I still looked. I saw a change in her also. She was thinner and had lost much of that heavenly spark that had before charmed me. But her gentleness and soft looks of compassion made her a more fit companion for one as miserable as I was.

The peace that I now felt did not last. Memory brought madness with it. When I thought of what had passed, a real insanity possessed me. Elizabeth alone could draw me from these fits. Her gentle voice would soothe me.

Soon after our arrival, my father spoke of my immediate marriage with Elizabeth. I remained silent.

"Have you, then, some other attachment?"

"No. I love Elizabeth, and I look forward to our marriage with delight. Let us set the date, and I will promise myself, in life or death, to her."

"My dear Victor, do not speak of death. Let us transfer our love for those we have lost to those who yet live. Our circle will be small, but it will be bound close by love. As time passes, new and dear objects of care will be born. These will replace those we have so cruelly lost."

Such were the lessons of my father. But I remembered the threat. Because of what I knew about the monster, I regarded him as unbeatable. When I remembered the words *"I shall be with you on your wedding night,"* I regarded my own death as unavoidable. But death was no evil to me. We decided that the ceremony should take place in ten days. This, I imagined, put the seal to my fate.

Great God! If I had known what the fiend was planning, I would have left my home forever. I would have wandered a friendless outcast over the earth rather than consent to this marriage. But the monster had blinded me to his real plans. When I thought that I had prepared only my own death, I hastened that of a far dearer victim.

As the date of our marriage grew nearer, I felt my heart sink within me. I hid my feelings as well as I could by an appearance of joy. I fooled my father, but I didn't fool Elizabeth. She looked forward to the marriage with calm contentment, mixed with a little fear. Past experience had taught her that what now appeared certain happiness might soon become an airy dream. It would leave no trace but deep and everlasting regret.

Preparations were made for the big day. Meanwhile, I took every precaution to defend my person in case the fiend should openly attack me. I carried pistols and a dagger at all times. Indeed, as the day approached, the threat seemed more like a dream, not to be taken seriously. The happiness I hoped for in my marriage seemed more certain.

On the day of the wedding, Elizabeth was melancholy.

Perhaps she was thinking of the secret that I had promised to tell her on the following day. My father was overjoyed, and he saw Elizabeth's mood as the shyness of a bride.

After the ceremony, we had a large party, and then Elizabeth and I left on our honeymoon. We would travel by boat, sleep that night at Evian,[2] and continue our voyage the next day.

The day was fair, the wind was favorable, and all smiled on our wedding trip. Those were the last moments of my life that I felt happy.

I took Elizabeth's hand and asked her why she seemed so sad. She said that she was bothered by a strange feeling that something was wrong. Then she said, "I will not listen to such a sinister voice. Look how beautiful the clouds and the mountains are! Look at the fish swimming in the clear waters! We can see every pebble that lies at the bottom. What a divine day! How happy and peaceful all nature appears!"

Thus Elizabeth tried to turn her thoughts and mine from all sad subjects. The sun was setting beneath the horizon as we landed. As I touched the shore, I felt those old cares and fears revive. These feelings were soon to clasp me and cling to me forever.

---

2. **Evian** a health spa and community in eastern France on Lake Geneva

12 The Creature's Final Revenge

It was eight o'clock when we landed. We walked for a short time on the shore and then retired to the inn. The wind rose with great violence in the west. The moon was beginning to descend. The clouds swept across it swifter than the flight of the vulture and dimmed her rays. Restless waves began to rise on the lake. Suddenly a heavy storm of rain fell.

I had been calm during the day, but as soon as night fell, a thousand fears arose in my mind. My right hand grasped a pistol hidden in my jacket. Every sound terrified me, but I resolved that I would fight the fiend to the death.

I passed an hour like this, and then I suddenly thought about how the coming struggle would frighten Elizabeth. To save her from having to witness it, I earnestly begged her to go to bed. I made up my mind not to join her until I found my enemy.

She left me, and I continued walking through the house, inspecting every corner that might be a hiding place to my enemy. I could find no trace of him. I was beginning to think that some lucky chance had prevented him from coming here. Suddenly, I heard a shrill and dreadful scream. It came from our room. As I heard it, the whole truth rushed into my mind. An instant later, the scream was repeated, and I rushed into the room.

Great God! Why did I not then die? Why am I here to talk about the destruction of the purest creature on earth? She was there, lifeless and inanimate, thrown across the bed. Her head was hanging down, and her pale face was half covered by her hair. Everywhere I turn, I see the same figure—her bloodless arms and relaxed form flung by the murderer on its bridal bier.[1] Could I see this, and live? Alas! Life is stubborn, and it clings closest where it is most hated. I fell senseless to the ground.

When I came to, I saw that I was surrounded by the people of the inn. Their faces showed breathless terror, but the horror of others was but a shadow of what I felt. I looked into the other room, where Elizabeth lay on the bed. Once again I gazed at Elizabeth, my love, my wife, so lately living, so dear, so worthy. She looked asleep. I rushed toward her and embraced her with passion. But the deadly coldness of her body told me that what I now held in my arms was no longer the Elizabeth I had loved. The mark of the fiend's grasp was on her neck.

Just then I happened to look up. The shutters had been opened, and with a sensation of horror, I saw at the open window the hideous and hated figure. A grin was on the face of the monster. He seemed to jeer as he pointed toward the corpse of my wife. I rushed to the window and, drawing my pistol, fired. But he eluded me, ran with the swiftness of lightning, and plunged into the lake.

The sound of the pistol brought a crowd into the room. For several hours we searched for him. Nets were cast into the lake, but in vain. Some thought he might have escaped into the woods, and a search party was sent. I tried to go with them, but I fell at last in a state of exhaustion. I was carried back to the inn.

A short time later I realized the danger my father

---

1. **bier** a stand on which a coffin or corpse is placed

and Ernest might be in. My father even now might be writhing under the fiend's grasp, and Ernest might be dead at his feet. I returned to Geneva with all possible speed.

My father and Ernest were still alive, but my father sank under the news I brought. He could not live with the horrors he had been forced to face. Within a few days, he died in my arms.

What then became of me? I know not. I lost all feeling. Chains and darkness were all I was aware of. I learned later that they called me mad and had locked me in a solitary cell.

As I awakened to reason, I also awakened to revenge. I felt a terrible rage when I thought of the monster I had created. I began to think of the best way to punish him. About a month after my release, I went to a criminal judge and told him the whole story. At first he didn't believe a word, but as I continued, he became more interested. When I finished my tale, I said, "This is the being whom I accuse. It is your duty to use your whole power to bring him to justice."

The judge had heard my story with that half kind of belief that is given to a tale of spirits and supernatural events. When I called upon him to act officially, I could tell by the way he talked that he didn't believe me. He knew that I had recently been locked up as a madman. He tried to soothe me as a nurse does a child. I left, angry and disturbed. The law, I could tell, would be no help. I decided that I had to plan another course of action.

My first plan was to leave Geneva forever. I took a sum of money and some jewels that had belonged to my mother and left.

My wanderings have taken me over a vast portion of the earth. These travels will end only when I die. I have endured every possible hardship that a traveler might meet. How I have lived I hardly know. The desire for revenge is all that has kept me alive. I dare not die and leave my enemy alive.

Before I left Geneva, I visited the cemetery where William, Elizabeth, and my father rested. I approached the tomb that marked their graves. Everything was silent except the leaves of the trees, which were gently moved by the wind. The night was dark, and the scene was solemn.

The deep grief I felt at first quickly gave way to rage and despair. They were dead, and I lived. Their murderer also lived, and to destroy him, I must continue my weary life. I knelt on the grass and kissed the earth. With quivering lips, I exclaimed, "I swear to pursue the fiend who caused this misery until he or I shall die in mortal conflict. For this purpose I will preserve my life. I call on you, spirits of the dead, to aid me in my work. Let the monster drink deep of agony. Let him feel the despair that now torments me."

I was answered through the stillness of night by a loud and fiendish laugh. It rang in my ears long and heavily. The mountains echoed it. I felt surrounded by mockery and laughter. The laughter died away, and I heard a well-known and hated voice, apparently close to my ear. It said, "I am satisfied, miserable wretch! You have decided to live, and I am satisfied."

I darted toward the sound, but the creature eluded me. Suddenly the moon arose and shone full upon his ghastly and deformed shape as he fled with more than mortal speed.

I pursued him, and for many months this has been my task. He leaves clues along the way to taunt me and to make sure I follow him. I have seen his footprints in the snow and other clues in the desert.

My life was indeed hateful to me. It was during sleep alone that I could taste joy. O blessed sleep! In sleep I saw my friends, my wife, and my beloved country. I saw the good face of my father, heard the silver tones of my Elizabeth's voice, and saw Clerval enjoying health and youth.

What the creature's feelings were I cannot know. Sometimes, indeed, he left marks in writing on the barks of trees, or cut in stone, that guided me. "My reign is not yet over," said one message. Another said, "Follow me. I seek the everlasting ices of the north. There you will feel the misery of cold and frost. Come, my enemy. We have yet to fight for our lives. Many hard and miserable hours must you endure before that fight begins."

I will never give up my search until he or I perish. As I journeyed north, the snows thickened. The cold increased, the rivers were covered with ice, and no fish could be caught. My enemy left another message: "Prepare! Your toils have just begun. Wrap yourself in furs and bring plenty of food. We shall soon go where your sufferings will satisfy my everlasting hatred."

I bought a sled and some dogs and thus traveled the snows with great speed. I was gaining on him, until I knew he was but one day's journey ahead of me. I met some people who lived in the cold regions, and got information about him. A gigantic monster, they said, had stolen their store of winter food, a sled, and some of their dogs. He had left, to their joy, in a direction that led to no land. They said that he would soon be destroyed by the breaking of the ice or frozen by the eternal frosts.

I do not know how many days have passed since then. Judging from the amount of food that is gone, it is probably about three weeks. Once, not too long ago, my eye caught a dark speck on the icy plain. I uttered a cry of joy when I saw the distorted figure of his well-known form. I drove the dogs as hard as I dared. After nearly two days, I saw my enemy no more than a mile away.

But now, my hopes were suddenly dashed. I lost all traces of him as the ice began to break up. After it split, with the mighty shock of an earthquake, the sea rolled between me and my enemy. I was left drifting on a scattered piece of ice. The ice was continually getting smaller, thus preparing for me a hideous death.

Many appalling hours passed, and several of my dogs died. It was then that I saw your vessel riding at anchor. I had no idea that vessels ever came so far north, and I was astounded at the sight. I quickly destroyed part of my sled to make oars, and so I was able to move my ice raft toward your ship.

If I had found out that you were heading south, I would have decided to trust myself to the seas rather than give up my purpose. I hoped you would give me a small boat with which I could pursue my enemy. But you were going north. You took me on board, and here we are.

If I die, swear to me, Walton, that he shall not escape. If he should appear, do not trust anything he says. His soul is full of treachery and evil. Do not listen to him. Think of William, Justine, Clerval, Elizabeth, my father, and of the wretched Victor. Then thrust your sword into his heart. I will be near, and I will direct the steel aright.

Closing Letters

You have read this strange and terrific story, Margaret. Does your blood not boil in horror? I believe what Frankenstein has said. The creature exists. The sight of the monster, which we saw from our ship, was enough proof. Sometimes I try to get from Frankenstein the details about how he made the monster, but on this point he is firm.

"Are you mad, my friend?" he asks. "Where would this lead you? Would you also create for yourself and the world such an enemy? Learn from my miseries. Do not seek to add to your own."

Frankenstein discovered that I had written notes about his story. He asked to see them, and then he corrected them in many places. Mainly, he gave life and spirit to the conversations he had held with his enemy. "Because you have written my story, I want to make sure it is accurate," he said.

It has been a week since he finished his story. I wish I could help him, but he doesn't want to live any longer. The only joy he looks forward to is to give his shattered spirit up to peace and death. He enjoys only one thing now. He believes that, when he sleeps, it is not just dreams that come to him but the beings themselves who visit him from a remote world.

Our talks are not always just about his own history and misfortunes. He knows a great deal about literature, and he speaks with great eloquence. What a glorious creature he must have been in earlier days! He seems to feel his own worth and the greatness of his fall.

"When younger," he said, "I believed I was destined for some great work. I believed that my talents might prove useful to my fellow creatures. But all my hopes have come to nothing. I have fallen, never, never again to rise."

I fear that Frankenstein will not live long. The only thing he is interested in is destroying the creature. Once that is accomplished, he wishes only to die.

September 2, 17—

My beloved Sister,

I write to you surrounded by danger and not knowing whether I shall ever see you or England again. I am closed in by mountains of ice that threaten every moment to crush my vessel. The crew looks to me for guidance, but I have none to give.

You will probably never receive this letter. You will never find out what happened to me. You will be waiting for my return. Years will pass, and you will not know whether to hope or despair. Oh! My beloved sister, this is more terrible to me than my own death. Heaven bless you and keep you happy!

September 5, 17—

Even though you will probably never read these papers, I must record what has happened. We are still surrounded by mountains of ice, still in danger of being crushed by them. The cold is excessive, and many of the crew have already died. Frankenstein's health is failing, and I do not think he will last long.

Today, six sailors came to my cabin. They had been

sent by the rest of the crew. They wanted me to promise that if the vessel should be freed from the ice, I would instantly turn the vessel southward. I did not give them an answer. I would rather die than return in shame, my purpose unfulfilled. Yet I do not feel that I can risk the lives of all my men for a cause that we may never accomplish.

September 12, 17—

It is settled. We are returning to England. I have lost my hopes of glory, and I have lost my friend. On September 9 the ice began to move. Roarings like thunder were heard in the distance as the island split and cracked in every direction. On the 11th the passage toward the south became perfectly free. When the sailors saw this, a shout of joy broke from them. Frankenstein, who was dozing, awoke and asked what all the noise was about. "They shout," I said, "because they will soon return to England."

"Do so, if you will, but I will not. I am weak, but surely my guiding spirits will give me strength." Saying this, he tried to get up from the bed, but the effort was too great for him. He fell back and fainted.

At length he opened his eyes. He breathed with difficulty and was unable to speak. The ship's doctor told me that he had only a few hours to live. I sat by the bed, watching him. Presently he spoke to me in a weak voice, saying, "Alas! I feel that I shall soon die, and he, my enemy, will still live. That he should live to be an instrument of evil disturbs me. Yet this hour is the only happy one I have enjoyed for several years. The forms of the beloved dead flit before me, and I rush to their arms. Farewell, Walton! Seek happiness in peace and avoid ambition. It leads only to misery."

His voice became fainter as he spoke. Finally his eyes closed forever. Margaret, what can I say about the death of this glorious spirit? My tears flow, and my mind is darkened by disappointment. But I journey toward England, and I may there find comfort.

I am interrupted. What are those sounds? It is midnight, the breeze blows fairly, and the watch on deck scarcely stirs. Again there is a sound as of a human voice, but hoarser. It comes from the cabin where the remains of Frankenstein still lie. I must arise and investigate. Good night, my sister.

Great God! What a scene has just taken place. It makes me dizzy to think about it. I hardly know if I have the power to write about it. Yet the tale that I have recorded would be incomplete without this final and wonderful catastrophe.

I entered the cabin where lay the remains of my ill-fated and admirable friend. Over him hung a form that I cannot find words to describe. He was gigantic, yet distorted in proportions. As he looked down, his face was hidden by long locks of ragged hair. One vast hand was extended. Its color and texture were like that of a mummy. When he heard me approaching, he stopped his exclamations of grief and horror and sprang toward the window. Never did I see a vision as horrible as his face. I tried to remember my duties concerning this destroyer. I called on him to stay.

He paused, looking on me with wonder. Turning toward the lifeless form of his creator, he appeared to forget my presence. Every feature and gesture seemed the result of some uncontrollable passion.

"That is also my victim!" he exclaimed. "In his murder, my crimes are finished. Oh, Frankenstein! Generous and devoted being! What good does it do that I now ask you to pardon me? I, who destroyed you by

destroying all that you loved. Alas! He is cold. He cannot answer me."

My first thought had been to obey Frankenstein's request to destroy his enemy. But now I felt a mixture of curiosity and compassion. I approached this tremendous being. I was finally able to say, "Being sorry now will do you no good. If you had listened to the voice of conscience earlier, Frankenstein would still be alive."

"Don't you think I was always sorry? Did you think that the groans of Clerval were music to my ears? My heart was made to feel love and sympathy. When it received only hatred, it suffered torture that you cannot even imagine.

"After the murder of Clerval, I returned, heartbroken, to Switzerland. I pitied Frankenstein. My pity amounted to horror. I felt a horror of myself. But when I discovered that he dared to hope for happiness, then envy and bitter rage filled me with a thirst for vengeance. I remembered my threat about his wedding night, and I resolved to carry it out.

"I knew that I was preparing for myself a deadly torture. But I was the slave, not the master, of an impulse that I detested but could not disobey. Yet when she died, I was not miserable! By then, I had cast off all feeling. From then on, evil became my good. The completion of my plan became a hungry passion. Now it is ended. There is my last victim!"

I was at first touched by his misery, but when I looked at the body of Frankenstein, rage rose up in me. "Wretch!" I cried. "The only thing you are sorry for is that your victim is now out of your power!"

"Oh, that is not true," he said. "I do not hope for any sympathy. Once I hoped to meet with beings who would love me for the excellent qualities that I was capable of expressing. I had high thoughts of honor and devotion. Now crime has degraded me beneath the lowest animal.

"You seem to know about my crimes and his misfortunes. However, his story told you nothing about the months of misery that I endured. For while I destroyed his hopes, I did not satisfy my own. Still I desired love and friendship, and I still was rejected. Am I to be thought the only criminal, when all humankind sinned against me? Why do you not hate Felix, who drove his friend from his door? Why do you not hate the man who shot me after I saved his child? No, I am to be spurned, kicked, and trampled. Even now my blood boils as I remember this injustice.

"It is true that I am a wretch. I have murdered the lovely and the helpless. I have strangled the innocent as they slept. I have pursued my creator to ruin. There he lies, white and cold in death. You hate me, but I hate myself even more.

"Fear not that I shall commit any more evil. My work is nearly complete. Neither you nor anyone else must die to accomplish that which must be done. Do not think that I shall be slow to perform this sacrifice. I shall leave your vessel on the ice raft that carried me here. I shall seek the most northern point of the globe. I shall collect my funeral pile and consume to ashes my miserable body. I shall die. I shall no longer feel the agonies that now consume me. Where can I find rest but in death?

"Farewell! I leave you and all of humankind. Farewell, Frankenstein! Soon I shall die. My ashes will be swept into the sea by the winds. My spirit will sleep in peace. Farewell."

He sprang from the cabin window to the ice raft that lay close to the vessel. He was soon carried away by the waves and lost in darkness and distance.

REVIEWING YOUR READING

Opening Letters

FINDING THE MAIN IDEA
1. The purpose of Robert Walton's voyage was to
(A) travel around the world (B) build character (C) be the first person to reach the North Pole (D) rescue lost travelers.

REMEMBERING DETAILS
2. Before the stranger boarded the ship, he asked
(A) where they were going (B) if the sailors had seen anyone else on the ice (C) where they were from (D) for some soup.

DRAWING CONCLUSIONS
3. The stranger looked out on the ice because
(A) he hoped to see the first dogsled that the crew had seen
(B) he liked the scenery (C) he was too bored in the cabin
(D) he never saw icebergs before.

USING YOUR REASON
4. If Robert Walton's ship hadn't been there, the stranger probably would have
(A) found another ship to rescue him (B) gone back the way he came (C) died (D) floated to safety.

THINKING IT OVER
5. Robert Walton told the stranger, "One man's life or death is but a small price to pay for the knowledge I am seeking." The stranger's reaction was to groan, cry, and say, "If you knew what I know, you would change your mind." What does this suggest to you about the kind of story the stranger would tell?

Chapter 1

FINDING THE MAIN IDEA
1. From an early age, Victor was interested in
(A) art (B) music (C) science (D) languages.

REMEMBERING DETAILS

2. Victor's father married
(A) his friend's sister (B) his servant (C) his childhood sweetheart (D) his friend's daughter.

DRAWING CONCLUSIONS

3. The troubles that Victor kept referring to probably had something to do with
(A) his father's public service (B) Henry Clerval's imagination (C) his study of science (D) the oak tree.

USING YOUR REASON

4. The peasant family agreed to let Victor's mother take care of Elizabeth because
(A) they didn't really like her (B) they thought that Elizabeth would be better off (C) Elizabeth didn't get along with their own children (D) they were paid.

THINKING IT OVER

5. What did Victor's mother and Elizabeth Lavenza have in common? To answer this question, think about the situations they were in before they were made part of the family and what might have happened to them if they had not been rescued from those situations.

Chapter 2

FINDING THE MAIN IDEA

1. Victor's great discovery while in college was
(A) how to win friends (B) electricity (C) the cause of life (D) why the sun shines.

REMEMBERING DETAILS

2. Victor's mother died of
(A) pneumonia (B) scarlet fever (C) polio (D) old age.

DRAWING CONCLUSIONS

3. Victor's creature was made of
(A) human body parts only (B) animal body parts only (C) human and animal body parts (D) bones, stones, and wood.

USING YOUR REASON

4. Victor's father was upset because Victor
(A) was spending too much money (B) hadn't written for so long (C) was getting bad grades (D) was ill.

THINKING IT OVER

5. Why was Victor so secretive about what he was doing? Use details from the story to support your answer.

Chapter 3

FINDING THE MAIN IDEA

1. Victor was horrified by the creature's
(A) appearance (B) cruelty (C) stupidity (D) strength.

REMEMBERING DETAILS

2. Victor had been working on the creature for
(A) five years (B) almost two years (C) a year
(D) several months.

DRAWING CONCLUSIONS

3. Victor's illness was the result of
(A) a bug bite (B) allergies (C) overwork and a feeling of despair (D) the creature's breathing on him.

USING YOUR REASON

4. One reason Victor studied languages with Clerval was that he
(A) had always enjoyed languages (B) wanted to read French poetry in the original (C) wanted to read the scientific works of some scientists from other countries (D) couldn't bear to think of studying science anymore.

THINKING IT OVER

5. Put yourself in the place of the creature moments after he was brought to life. What might have been going through his mind? Why do you think that he came to Victor's room? After Victor ran away, what do you think the creature did?

Chapter 4

FINDING THE MAIN IDEA

1. Chapter 4 is mainly about

(A) the evidence against Justine (B) the loss of William and Justine (C) Elizabeth's testimony (D) William's funeral.

REMEMBERING DETAILS

2. William disappeared when he was
    (A) playing hide-and-seek with Ernest (B) swimming
    (C) sailing a boat (D) fishing.

DRAWING CONCLUSIONS

3. Victor probably said nothing about the creature during Justine's trial because
    (A) he knew that nobody would believe him (B) he thought that she'd be found innocent (C) nobody asked him
    (D) he wanted Justine to pay for William's death.

USING YOUR REASON

4. Victor was convinced that the creature killed William because
    (A) he saw him do it (B) the marks on William's neck were from a huge hand (C) the creature told him that he did it
    (D) he just had a strong feeling about it.

THINKING IT OVER

5. Why do you think that Mary Shelley used the name *Justine* for the character who was so unjustly accused of William's murder?

Chapter 5

FINDING THE MAIN IDEA

1. Another good title for this chapter would be
    (A) A Meeting on the Mountain (B) A House of Mourning
    (C) Victor's Hatred Grows (D) The View from the Top.

REMEMBERING DETAILS

2. Victor's father tried to encourage Victor to
    (A) go back to school (B) visit William's grave (C) take up the study of music (D) get on with life.

DRAWING CONCLUSIONS

3. Victor traveled to the valley of Chamounix and climbed the mountain because he
    (A) planned to jump (B) wanted to die in an avalanche

(C) found natural beauty a comfort and an escape from his troubles (D) wanted to get away from his family.

USING YOUR REASON

4. Another way to ask the creature's question, "How dare you sport thus with life?" might be
(A) "How can you take life so lightly?" (B) "How can you risk your life by climbing mountains?" (C) "How can you dare to risk fighting against me?" (D) "Do you think life is just a game?"

THINKING IT OVER

5. Compare Frankenstein's first reactions to the creature to some of his later reactions. Why do you think he behaved as he did?

Chapter 6

FINDING THE MAIN IDEA

1. When people saw the creature, they reacted with
(A) love (B) kindness (C) interest (D) fear.
2. The creature's actions concerning the cottagers show that he was
(A) kind (B) angry (C) dangerous (D) sneaky.

REMEMBERING DETAILS

3. The people who lived in the cottage were
(A) father, mother, and son (B) uncle, niece, and nephew
(C) father, son, and daughter (D) friends.
4. The creature's main task at this time was to learn
(A) how to walk (B) the language (C) to dance
(D) how to cook.

DRAWING CONCLUSIONS

5. We know that the cottagers were poor because
(A) they often went hungry (B) the old man was blind
(C) they lived in the country (D) they didn't have a large house.

USING YOUR REASON

6. Felix probably read to the old man and Agatha
(A) to put them to sleep (B) to hear his own voice
(C) to punish them (D) to entertain them.

7. When the creature entered one of the cottages in the village, why do you think that the villagers chased him away, throwing rocks and other things at him?

Chapter 7

FINDING THE MAIN IDEA

1. Safie came to the cottage because she
(A) needed a job (B) had no place else to live (C) wanted to get some French lessons (D) loved Felix.

REMEMBERING DETAILS

2. Felix met Safie
(A) while planning her father's escape from jail (B) in school (C) at the marketplace (D) through mutual friends.

3. The reason the De Laceys no longer lived in France was that they
(A) were tired of France (B) wanted to see more of the world (C) were exiled (D) lost their visas.

DRAWING CONCLUSIONS

4. If Safie's father had known that she was planning to find Felix and marry him, he'd have
(A) helped her (B) gone with her (C) stopped her from going (D) bought her a wedding dress.

USING YOUR REASON

5. The creature's reaction to hearing about the fate of America's original inhabitants showed that he was
(A) silly (B) sensitive (C) hardhearted (D) jealous.

THINKING IT OVER

6. The creature heard about the various relationships that bind human beings to one another. Then he realized that he had no mother, father, brother, or sister. Who was the one person in the world to whom the creature was connected? Why do you think he could claim the right to be loved and protected by that person?

Chapter 8

FINDING THE MAIN IDEA

1. The creature wanted Victor to provide him with a
   (A) mate (B) house (C) teacher (D) family.

2. The creature approached the old man first because the old man was
   (A) blind (B) courageous (C) weak (D) kind.

REMEMBERING DETAILS

3. The creature saved a girl from
   (A) a fire (B) starvation (C) drowning (D) a bear.

DRAWING CONCLUSIONS

4. The creature placed the miniature in the folds of Justine's clothing in order to
   (A) surprise her (B) hide it (C) confuse her (D) cause blame to fall on her.

USING YOUR REASON

5. The creature learned quickly. This seems to indicate that
   (A) he had nothing else to do (B) he was highly intelligent
   (C) Felix was a good teacher (D) the lessons were very easy.

THINKING IT OVER

6. Think about the creature's request for a mate. Do you think that Frankenstein should have fulfilled this request? Explain why or why not.

Chapter 9

FINDING THE MAIN IDEA

1. Victor postponed the wedding so that he could
   (A) have more fun (B) create a mate for the creature
   (C) save some money (D) go back to college.

REMEMBERING DETAILS

2. The creature promised to live in
   (A) England (B) South America (C) Africa (D) France.

DRAWING CONCLUSIONS
3. If Victor broke his promise, the creature would probably
(A) cry (B) leave town (C) hurt someone (D) not care.

USING YOUR REASON
4. Victor could not enjoy the trip to England as much as Clerval did because
(A) he had too much on his mind (B) he had been there before (C) he was ill (D) he missed Elizabeth.

THINKING IT OVER
5. Why did Victor think it was safe to leave his family unprotected while he stayed in England?

Chapter 10

FINDING THE MAIN IDEA
1. The creature became enraged when Victor
(A) went to Scotland (B) took too long to finish his work
(C) destroyed his work (D) set out for Perth.

REMEMBERING DETAILS
2. Victor's greatest fear was that the two creatures
(A) would hate each other (B) would produce children
(C) would kill him (D) would hurt his family.

DRAWING CONCLUSIONS
3. The people who met Victor on the beach thought that he might be a
(A) murderer (B) scientist (C) thief (D) reporter.

USING YOUR REASON
4. Victor had forebodings of evil because he
(A) knew the future (B) always thought the worst
(C) knew what had happened before (D) had a dream.

THINKING IT OVER
5. The creature threatened to be with Victor on his wedding night. Why do you think he mentioned that particular night rather than any other night?

Chapter 11

FINDING THE MAIN IDEA

1. Victor's illness followed his realization that
    (A) a stranger killed Clerval (B) the creature killed Clerval
    (C) he might be next (D) he was accused of Clerval's murder.

REMEMBERING DETAILS

2. Victor was found innocent because he was
    (A) insane (B) too weak to do it (C) Clerval's friend (D) not
    in the area when the crime was committed.

DRAWING CONCLUSIONS

3. Victor went ahead with the wedding because
    (A) he wanted to face the creature and get what he thought
    would be their final meeting over with (B) Elizabeth insisted
    (C) his father insisted (D) he needed a vacation.

USING YOUR REASON

4. Part of the reason Elizabeth was melancholy was that
    (A) she really didn't want to get married (B) she sensed
    Victor's apprehensions (C) she had seen the creature (D) the
    weather had been bad.

THINKING IT OVER

5. The creature never said that he would kill Victor. What made
    Victor think that he was in danger?

Chapter 12

FINDING THE MAIN IDEA

1. The next two people to die were
    (A) Victor and Elizabeth (B) Elizabeth and Victor's father
    (C) Elizabeth and Ernest (D) Victor and Walton.

REMEMBERING DETAILS

2. Just before the ice broke up, Victor had been
    (A) about a day behind the creature (B) two days behind the
    creature (C) about a mile from the creature (D) ready
    to give up.

DRAWING CONCLUSIONS

3. It was obvious from the creature's actions that he
   (A) wanted to get away from Victor (B) wanted to have a showdown with Victor (C) was sorry for what he did (D) wanted to help Victor.

USING YOUR REASON

4. The creature had a better chance of survival than Victor because
   (A) he was so strong (B) he had a better dogsled (C) he had more food (D) he had more reason to live.

THINKING IT OVER

5. Why do you think that the creature led Victor on such a chase?

Closing Letters

FINDING THE MAIN IDEA

1. The creature's plan was to kill himself by
   (A) drowning (B) starvation (C) freezing (D) fire.

REMEMBERING DETAILS

2. The creature said that after the death of Clerval, he felt
   (A) satisfaction (B) heartbroken (C) rage (D) justified.

DRAWING CONCLUSIONS

3. We can assume that the creature became an evil monster because of
   (A) the way Victor made him (B) the way he was treated (C) poor diet (D) an illness he suffered.

USING YOUR REASON

4. Walton turned the vessel around before reaching the North Pole because
   (A) it was too dangerous to continue (B) he didn't want to run into the creature (C) he missed his sister (D) someone else was already there.

THINKING IT OVER

5. In her book *Frankenstein,* what do you think Mary Shelley was saying about human beings and the way we treat one another?